HELL HATH NO FURY

HELL HATH NO FURY

BRYNA TAUBMAN

ST. MARTIN'S

Dedicated to all children who become weapons in adult divorce wars

Acknowledgments

Third Thursday Group, San Diego County Library California Room, *San Diego Reader*, *San Diego Tribune*, *Los Angeles Times*, Court TV, Kirstin Cleveland of NPR Public Information, Kerry Wells, and Jack Earley, plus the friends and relatives who offered encouragement and support.

PROLOGUE

THE TOTAL QUIET OF AN AFFLUENT NEIGHBORHOOD IN THE STILLNESS OF
a Sunday morning in early November enveloped Cypress Avenue,
a block-long street just above the northwest hook of San Diego's
Balboa Park. Suddenly, five gunshots ripped through the silence.
Those five reports marked the violent end to one of the bitterest
divorces in the town's recent memory and the start of an even more
notorious criminal case.

The savagery that shattered the early morning quiet had been predicted by several people, including those most nearly involved, but
no one had really believed it would happen. The gunshots were the
final eruption of long-simmering rage and humiliation, fueled by
fears, some real and some imagined, and a sense of desperation.

Some people said later the shooting was a vicious, premeditated
act; others argued it was provoked, the result of a malicious campaign
to undermine and discredit a woman who had been grievously
wounded. Its outcome left two people dead, four children orphaned,
and a town divided.

1

SHOTS IN THE DARK

ABOUT FIVE A.M. ON NOVEMBER 5, 1989, A WHITE CHEVROLET SUBURBAN van turned onto the empty street and stopped at the two-story brick house near the end of Cypress Avenue. The curved driveway passed in front of the four white columns that rose to the overhanging roof; the two in the center framed the pediment-topped front door. White shutters decorated the second-story windows, and two wings covered in white clapboard grew from the central structure. The Georgian-style mansion seemed out of place next to the more traditionally California outlines of its tile-roofed neighbors in the tiny enclave of wealth known as Marston Hills.

But that seemed to be the point for the house's owner, Daniel T. Broderick III, a medical malpractice attorney and a major figure in San Diego legal circles. A dashing dresser who wore only custom-tailored suits and had a top hat and cape for more formal occasions, he identified with the mansion's Southern plantation aura of red brick, double chimneys, and columns. The big house represented success to Broderick, at least as he had defined it years earlier—"mansions, cars, and boats"—to his first wife.

Elisabeth Anne Broderick, known as Betty to her friends, emerged from the Suburban dressed in casual clothes and a diamond necklace

3

and earrings. She walked to the front door. A tall, slightly overweight woman with a puffy face, she wore her blond hair pulled back into a ponytail. She peered through the door's glass side panels to the dark interior. She looked like a suburban matron, but her stealthy movements were those of a burglar, checking for signs of life inside the big house.

She clutched an almost comically large key in one hand and tried it in the lock. Her other hand hung down by her side, as if she were gripping something heavy. When the door wouldn't open, Betty turned to the back of the house. The back door was more cooperative, and she entered quietly. She was inside without a sound to break the stillness.

Upstairs in the master bedroom above the front door, no sense of impending violence disturbed the sleep of Dan Broderick and his bride of seven months, Linda Kolkena Broderick. They had spent Saturday on the water with friends, on Dan's powerboat. Fresh air and salt spray are terrific soporifics. He wore only undershorts in the cool San Diego night, but Linda was dressed more warmly in pajamas. He slept on the side of the double bed nearest the door that led to the stair landing. In the relatively small room, he was also closest to the wall.

The closed door of their bedroom faced Betty Broderick at the top of the stairs. Undaunted, she walked down the hall, going through the open doorway of another room closer to the back of the house. She knew the small TV room led to a bathroom adjoining the master bedroom. From that doorway she would be inside before Dan knew she was there. It was part of her plan that he have no warning of her presence.

Pushing on the door from the bathroom, Betty Broderick stepped into the bedroom. Drapes covered the window, keeping the brightness of the dawn out of the room. She could see only the vaguest shapes of furniture and people. Two years later she wept as she recounted the next few seconds of that morning:

"The door to their bedroom was partially open
. . . it wasn't closed . . . like ajar . . . the mo-

tion I made, although I don't think it was a big
motion, the movement I made into their bedroom
woke them up and they moved. Somebody
screamed: 'Call the police!' and I said, 'No!' I just
fired the gun and this big noise went off and then I
grabbed the phone and got the hell out of there. But
I wasn't in that room . . . it was just an explosion.
I moved, they moved, the gun went off it was like
Aaahhh!!! . . . it was that fast."

That fast and one explosion, set off by a slight movement, perhaps a
scream. Betty Broderick is the only one left alive to tell the story. She
remembers only one explosion, but the gun fired five times. Three of
the hollow-point bullets hit the two people on the bed. The police
found two more bullet holes, one in the wall beyond the bed and one
embedded in a bedside table.

Betty Broderick insisted she didn't remember pulling the trigger
five times or even aiming the revolver she was holding. The curtained
room was dark, the furniture only "dim shapes," and she didn't recall
seeing the pair on the bed, just what she described as "an impression" of someone on the mattress near the door as she entered the
bedroom. Questioned about those seconds, Broderick explained she
had visual memories, like slides, but some of them are blank:

". . . I remember opening the door to the bedroom, so I see myself doing that, but then, I don't
see anything else . . . I know I grabbed the phone,
but I don't remember leaving the house or running
down the stairs or anything, so it's like there are
these spots missing. It's like a flash of this and then
she's over there and a flash of that . . ."

Betty thought she remembered someone screaming, but could not
be sure if it was Linda yelling "Call the police," or her own anguished
howl. "I just went *Aaagghhh*!! I felt like I made a huge scream, but I
don't know if I made any noise. It was just—just all sensation. I

moved in and they moved . . . then there was this huge explosion and scream and everything all at once."

Her next visual memory puts her on the other side of the bed, by Dan and the door that led to the stairs and the front door: "I'm grabbing the phone so he couldn't get on it. I tried to get out of the room, and it kind of jerked and I jerked it back and pulled it out of the wall, and I think I threw it on the top of the stairs."

Behind her, she left Linda Kolkena Broderick sprawled facedown across the double bed, twisted in the bloodstained sheets. One bullet hit the twenty-eight-year-old woman in the chest, a second in the head, killing her instantly. Dan Broderick lay on the floor next to the wall, half under the bed. He had a bullet wound in his upper back that penetrated his lung. Seventeen days before his forty-fifth birthday, he died a few minutes after he was shot, still trying to reach the nightstand phone that had been snatched from his grasp.

The prosecutor in *California* v. *Broderick,* Kerry Wells, described the deaths of Dan and Linda as "cold-blooded murder." A long-time deputy district attorney in San Diego County and head of the Domestic Violence Bureau, Wells acknowledged no rationalization or provocation for Betty Broderick's actions on that morning in early November, and the lawyer maintained a cold fury as she prosecuted the case for more than two years.

Broderick herself never denied firing the fatal shots, although she always insisted she did not remember pulling the trigger. She contended the emotional and psychological abuse that she endured during sixteen years of marriage and four years of divorce from Dan Broderick had turned her into "an electrified crazy person" and drove her to desperate, violent actions.

Betty's defense attorney, Jack Earley, argued that her crime was manslaughter, not murder; the distinction could mean the difference between life in prison without parole and a sentence of fifteen years. It was an improbable alternative for a woman who once thought her future included nothing more threatening than climbing the ladders of social success in the country clubs of La Jolla and the ballrooms of San Diego.

2

THE FUGITIVE

UNSURE IF SHE HAD HIT ANYONE IN THE DARK PANIC OF DAN AND LINDA'S bedroom, Betty Broderick ran down the stairs and out the front door in the silence that followed the gun blasts. She was convinced that Dan was even then calling the police to have her arrested, and, terror-stricken, she drove off as quickly as she could.

"I had nowhere to go," Broderick testified at her trials. "I was afraid that Dan was after me. I was afraid when I went into that house of confronting Dan, and then when I left I thought he was after me."

She said she did not remember driving away from the Broderick house in Marston Hills, nor could she recall how she came to be heading back toward her own home in La Jolla. The most obvious and easiest route for a driver as familiar with the area as Betty Broderick begins on the Cabrillo Freeway just a few blocks from Dan's house. That major San Diego highway connects to the Camino Del Rio which goes west and meets Interstate 5.

I-5 is also known as the San Diego Freeway, the coastal highway that runs south from Los Angeles and divides the older shore communities from the newer inland developments in the mountains to the east. It is the fastest route between Cypress Avenue in central San

Diego and Betty's home near the Scripps Institute of Oceanography. Somewhere along the way back home she became worried that the police would be looking for her at her house, frightening her two young sons.

That morning, Danny Jr., thirteen, and ten-year-old Rhett were asleep in her home on Calle del Cielo about ten miles away, but that was only temporary. After a long and nasty divorce in which Dan emerged victorious in every court action, he had full custody of the boys, and Betty complained bitterly and unendingly to everyone she knew, accusing him of stealing her children.

"I thought, 'Oh man, you can't go home,' because he's going to have called the police, and the police are going to be waiting at my house. I didn't want to scare the boys and everything. So I ended up at a phone booth in Clairemont," she recalled for the jury.

Apparently turning off the San Diego Freeway, she stopped at a gas station in the next community inland from La Jolla. She recalled making one call. "I only remember dialing," Betty said, "and calling and talking to Dian Black."

Black, another woman who had been through a bitter divorce, testified in court about a "rambling, disoriented" call from Betty, who seemed to be "in shock."

"I need help," were the first words Dian Black heard.

A short, attractive woman with shoulder-length dark hair, bangs, and glasses when she testified at the second trial, Dian had known Betty Broderick for about two years when the phone rang early that Sunday morning. They had become close friends over the shared experiences of their divorces, and had supported each other through several emotional crises. This would be something else.

"[She] sounded like she was crying," Black recalled. Broderick was also "rambling about something that just happened." The call became even more bizarre because Betty would "start talking really fast, then stop."

Her rambling sounded "incoherent" to Black. "She said she had just come from Dan and Linda's house. She said she fired a gun. It was dark and she didn't know whether she hit anybody . . .

"The concept of her going over there and having committed anything over there, whether it was just to confront Dan, was so shocking to me, I didn't believe it. Confrontations I understood were in court."

Black wanted to know where Betty was calling from but her friend could provide only the vaguest clues to her whereabouts:

> "She thought it was Clairemont. I asked specifically and she couldn't tell me. I asked her to look around and identify the building, the restaurants and gas stations. From the things she was describing, I could figure out where she was. She read me the phone number. I told her to stay put. I'd call back right away . . . [she was] not to leave the phone until someone calls her."

At first Black thought Betty was having "a nervous breakdown," but she also feared the emotionally distraught woman might really have confronted Dan Broderick. Dian knew Betty's friend Brad Wright would be asleep at the house on Calle del Cielo in La Jolla with the Broderick boys. She called and told him about the unsettling phone call from Betty.

Betty herself was too nervous to wait alone at the gas station for Dian to call her back. Convinced that Dan had reached the police, and aware that the distinctive LODEMUP vanity plates on the Suburban made her easy to find, she called her younger daughter.

Estranged from her father when she dropped out of high school and briefly coped with a drug problem, the eighteen-year-old Lee lived in Pacific Beach with her boyfriend, Jason Prantil. It was shortly after seven in the morning when the phone rang in the small apartment that the young couple shared on Sapphire Street.

In emotionally wrenching testimony, Lee recalled that early Sunday morning conversation with her mother for jurors at both trials:

"She said she was in trouble and needed my help . . . She told me she shot my dad; she shot the son of a bitch and wanted to come to my house."

Betty testified that she hadn't wanted to involve Lee in her troubles, but "Dan didn't know where Lee lived . . . so if he was sending the cops to get me, he couldn't send them to Lee's house because he didn't know where Lee lived. Nobody knew where Lee lived, except me."

The rest of that call Lee remembered as being "pretty hysterical." Her mother talked about taking her own life, the teenager said, but "there weren't any bullets in her gun." Betty recalled telling her daughter that she would be right over, but she had added, "If I don't arrive, honey, it's because the police got me."

When her mother hung up, Lee tried to call her father at home, she said, but "I picked up the phone to call and remembered I don't know the number there. My dad had a separate line in his room and his office . . . and I was not allowed to know the number."

Unable to reach her father, the young woman waited with Jason for Betty to arrive. When she walked in, Lee was shocked at her mother's condition.

"Her voice was trembling," Lee testified. "She was talking very fast, walking around the room, and she wouldn't sit still . . . She told me that she thought she shot Dad, but didn't know because it was dark and the drapes were drawn. She wasn't sure."

Uncertain whether to believe her mother or not, Lee asked if anyone was hurt, if there had been any blood or screams. She remembered her mother saying that "she didn't think she had hurt my dad because he sat up and said, 'Okay, you shot me. I'm dead.' " Then, Lee recalled, Betty said she pulled the phone from the wall and ran away.

"She said she couldn't go on like this anymore," Lee testified.

Jason Prantil also remembered a woman who was clearly distraught that November morning.

"She wasn't making a lot of sense," he told the jury. "She looked like she had been up for a couple days. She looked like she was sick, like she was panic-stricken."

Betty insisted that Dan had called the police and that they would be looking for her car. She wanted Lee and Jason to drive her to the police station so she could surrender. Trying to calm her nearly frantic mother, Lee made a cup of tea for Betty, who took one sip and ran retching to the bathroom.

In fact, the police were just then getting to the house on Cypress Avenue. When Dian Black called Brad Wright, he wasn't sure what to do. He considered calling the police himself but was worried about the young Broderick boys. Instead, Wright called Brian Forbes, a lawyer who was a good friend of Dan's and who lived close to Betty in La Jolla.

Forbes and his wife Gail were having coffee when Wright called about seven that morning. Explaining that Betty had called Dian and that the story was secondhand, Wright was still anxious, and suggested that he and Brian drive into San Diego to check on Dan and Linda.

While Gail Forbes went to stay with the Broderick boys, Forbes dialed the house in Marston Hills. When no one answered, he called both an ambulance and the police, but, he told the jury, "They didn't believe me."

Wright drove to Cypress Avenue with Brian, giving him directions to the nearly inaccessible blocks of large homes tucked into a corner overlooking Balboa Park. They found the front and back doors of the Broderick house locked. Forbes, an athletically built man in his thirties, noticed an open window, and after tearing through the screen, climbed over the washer and dryer into the laundry room.

Concerned he would be mistaken for an intruder, Brian yelled a warning to Dan and Linda. There was no response, and he ran up the stairs "two at a time as fast as I could." He found the door to the bedroom open and a gruesome scene in front of him.

"I felt Dan's throat for a pulse . . . he was cold," Forbes remembered. "I felt a presence behind me. Brad said, 'They're both dead.'" The lawyer testified that he also remembered seeing what he described as "a pool of vomit [that] looked like cookies-and-cream ice cream."

On the landing, the two men spotted the telephone trailing the wires that Betty Broderick had ripped from the wall and dropped there. They ran down the stairs to use the cellular phone in Wright's car to call the police. As the pair walked out the front door, a patrol car pulled up.

Betty, sure the police had been alerted much earlier, was contacting her friends and family before surrendering. Lee had called her sister Kim, a college student in Tucson. Kim was a year older and less alienated from Dan Broderick than her younger sister. At the trials, she remembered the call from Lee that came "before eight" that Sunday morning:

"She said that Mom was there and that she had shot Dad and Linda . . . I talked to Mom. I asked what happened. She said she shot them, but she wasn't sure if she hit anybody. She said, 'You know I had to do it. I couldn't let him live. It was one or the other.'"

After talking to her oldest daughter, Betty Broderick asked Lee and Jason to check on the younger boys. She also wanted her telephone book and keys, and told Lee where to look for them in her house in La Jolla. The shingle-sided house sat on a hillside cul-de-sac with a view of the Pacific.

When Lee arrived, Rhett was riding his bike on the empty street. She went inside to look in the pewter cup on the mantel for the keys and in the kitchen for the phone book, but could find neither in the locations Betty had suggested. When she went back outside to talk to her little brother, Lee became aware that "the police were hiding in the bushes of the next-door neighbor's house."

She recalled what happened next: "They came out and asked if I'd seen my mother. I said no. They asked what I was doing there. I said I was getting my laundry. I went back inside, got my laundry, and left."

Lee and Jason drove back to Sapphire Street and found that Betty had not been idle. While they were gone, she had been speaking with friends, telling them what happened and making plans.

One of those she phoned was Patti Monahan. Another divorcée, Monahan was a longtime friend of Betty's and knew the particulars of the long battle with Dan, but the graphic details she heard that Sunday morning horrified her.

In court a year later she could no longer recall exactly what Betty had said to her. Monahan did remember that she had repeated the vivid comments to her boyfriend, Jerry Thatcher, right after hanging up the phone.

Thatcher was less delicate. He remembered "very clearly" what

Patti had said about her conversation: "Betty has really flipped out this time. She says she shot Dan."

Testifying at the first trial, Thatcher recalled Monahan telling him that Betty said she "shot him five times. He was gurgling in his own blood. It's true, they really do shit in their pants."

(After his testimony, both attorneys agreed to a stipulation for the jury, explaining that Dan Broderick did not lose bowel control before he died. The two lawyers would also agree later that it was impossible for Betty to have heard anything after firing five shots in the small bedroom. Her comments that Broderick "gurgled" or sat up and said "you shot me" may also have been things she imagined.)

After the call to Patti Monahan, Broderick dialed her parents, then living in Eastchester, New York. Betty was talking to her father when Lee and Jason came home. Frank Bisceglia testified to the brief but disturbing phone call from his daughter that Sunday morning: "She was sobbing, she was very hysterical."

A small, ruddy-faced man, the seventy-seven-year-old contractor testified that she had said: "Dan is driving me crazy. He's driving me up the wall. I feel like committing suicide."

The Catholic father who had sent all six of his children to parochial schools seemed troubled to be repeating his daughter's conversation. It was a brief call, Bisceglia said, probably less than two minutes, and Betty never mentioned shooting Dan and Linda Broderick.

Lee also testified her mother was more distressed than ever after speaking to her parents in New York. The younger woman said that she tried to reach the therapist that Betty had been seeing but couldn't locate him.

Reiterating her decision to surrender, Betty took off her diamond necklace and earrings and her watch and put them on Lee. She reported that two friends had agreed to come with her to the police. They had made plans to meet in the parking lot of a local restaurant, and Jason agreed to take her there.

Dian Black was waiting with Ronnie Brown, another woman who had come into Betty's life since her divorce. Jason drove them toward the La Jolla police station. Black recalled an uncomfortable ride.

Betty was "disoriented, confused . . . she would ramble on . . . The rest of us were pretty hysterical, trying to calm her down."

At other times Black said Broderick seemed to be almost in a trance—"not physically there." They were in front of the police station, but before Betty could get out, Dian and Ronnie convinced her to speak with a lawyer first. Broderick agreed and a new plan was made.

Lee remembered it was Dian Black who suggested that some of the legal papers relating to the Broderick divorce battles might be important. The boxed files were already stored at Betty's newly purchased condominium, the apartment that was replacing the larger, more expensive Calle del Cielo house. Under the new plans, Lee and Jason would go to the condo while Betty talked to an attorney. She told Lee where to find the box of files she might need.

Using the back of a photograph she found on the floor of the car, Broderick jotted some other instructions for Lee—the name of the woman who helped her with financial records and the combination to the locked storage bin in the garage at her house. She also wrote a will, and Lee recalled the details of that: "She had Dian and Ronnie sign. She left everything she had to my brothers and sister and I. That's all she wrote in the car."

Lee and Jason left, dropping the three women in front of a telephone booth so they could call a lawyer. The young couple drove to the condominium to pick up the papers Betty wanted. Lee found the right box quickly, and they were leaving when a police car arrived. It was Lee's second run-in with police that morning, and this time she wasn't as lucky.

"On the way out of the driveway from the condo, the police pulled in. They told us to get out of our car and to get in the back of their car," Lee remembered. She returned to her apartment again, this time with a police escort, to find a message from her mother on the answering machine.

The young woman told the jury how she listened to the message with a detective who then confiscated the tape. She heard it again in court when it was played for the jury:

"It's 11:05. I have an appointment with an attorney at eleven-thirty. We're going there. Don't worry, sweetie. Everything will be okay. I hope you're okay . . . Thank goodness you have the machine on."

The detective also picked up Betty Broderick's big leather purse, left in Lee's apartment. When the police officer looked inside, he found a .38-caliber handgun.

A few hours later Betty Broderick, accompanied by attorney Ronald Frant, surrendered to the San Diego police in the deaths of her ex-husband and his new wife.

Somehow, a marriage that had begun with all of the bright promise of the American dream had turned into a nightmare more horrific than anyone could have imagined. Certainly none of it could have been foretold twenty-three years earlier, when the thin, studious college senior from Pittsburgh first noticed the bright-haired Italian-American girl from the suburbs of New York.

BAREFOOT IN THE PARK

T HEY MET CUTE, EVEN BY HOLLYWOOD STANDARDS, AT A FOOTBALL WEEK-end at Notre Dame in 1965.

Elisabeth Anne (Betty) Bisceglia, seventeen years old and a freshman at the all-woman Catholic College of Mount St. Vincent in New York City, had come west with a couple of classmates to South Bend, Indiana, for the annual big game between the Fighting Irish and the University of Southern California Trojans.

At a typically raucous college party that Saturday night, a bespectacled, serious-faced senior asked to borrow Betty's pen. The perky blonde with big blue eyes watched as the young man introduced himself by writing his name on the table cloth: Daniel T. Broderick III MD (A).

"I asked him why the parenthesis," Betty recalled a quarter of a century later. "He said that he had just been accepted into medical school, so it stood for Daniel T. Broderick the Third, M.D. almost. I thought it was funny."

Betty remembered the party and her meeting with Dan Broderick in detail, and her voice grew animated as she described it for a jury: "It was a very, very loud, very rowdy party. Jerry Lee Lewis himself was just to my right. It was really noisy and really crowded. It was hard to have a conversation."

Talking to *Los Angeles Times* reporter Amy Wallace after her arrest, Betty recalled how Dan looked that first Saturday night: "He had long skinny sideburns, round tortoiseshell glasses. You're talking geek city." He was also nearly an inch shorter than the five-foot-ten athletic Betty, and she wasn't that impressed with the pale young man from the Midwest.

She bragged about her conquest years later, though. According to her, Dan told his college friends that he had met the girl he wanted to marry and it was Betty.

In the middle of their bitter divorce more than twenty years after the memorable weekend, Broderick reportedly denied he had been infatuated then with the woman he was now rejecting. But he was interested enough in 1965 to pursue her long distance.

Dan had been accepted at Cornell Medical School in New York, and he jokingly made a date with Betty for the following September so she could show him around the city. At her trial, she would recall that they planned to rendezvous at a New York City landmark immortalized as a meeting place by Holden Caulfield in J. D. Salinger's *Catcher in the Rye*—the clock at the Biltmore Hotel near Grand Central Station: "I said I'd meet him at the clock at a certain day and a certain time."

For the rest of his senior year at Notre Dame, Dan sent Betty first telegrams, then letters. She remembered that she had ignored the telegrams but responded to the letters. Still, when the day came to meet him at the Biltmore clock, "I was scared and didn't go," Betty recalled.

A determined Dan Broderick was not to be denied. He phoned to learn why she had stood him up and he made another date with her. By then Betty was a little more interested in the ambitious young man who seemed so very self-assured.

Dan Broderick's stubborn, romantic pursuit also appealed to the pop culture fantasies of love and marriage and a traditional fairy-tale ending that Betty had grown up with. After twelve years in all-girl parochial schools, her experience with boys and dating was limited.

But she had the examples of her parents and their friends of what life would hold for a beautiful, bright Catholic girl: marriage, a large family, and a home in the suburbs with all the miracles of modern technology.

Asked in court what she had expected of a husband, Betty replied: "To be nice and be supportive and to be the father of my children. I thought that we'd live happily ever after."

Growing up in a Westchester County bedroom community north of New York City, and the third of six children in an Italian-American family, Betty Bisceglia had all the abundance of a large, close-knit home filled with loving relatives. Her father was a building contractor in New York and they lived well. Betty and her brothers and sisters went to Catholic schools and spent weekends and summers swimming and playing tennis and golf at the local country club, dressed in the latest *Villager* styles.

"My mom's real social," Betty told reporters for the *San Diego Reader* in a 1988 interview for a story about her marriage and divorce. "We had lots of clothes and designer things.

"I had a maid when I was growing up. Not that she was a slave. But our house ran very smoothly. I don't remember my mother scrubbing floors, if you get the picture. My laundry magically got done. I don't remember who did it, but I know I didn't."

With all the comforts of her childhood home, that's where Betty stayed while she attended college. And that's where she was living when she began dating Dan Broderick in the fall of 1966 as he started his first year of medical school in upper Manhattan and she entered her sophomore year at Mt. St. Vincent, not far away in the Bronx.

Dan, too, seemed to embody the American success story: the eldest of five boys and four girls in an Irish-Catholic family, his father used discipline learned in the Navy to keep the brood in line. "Our will to succeed is inherited; it's genetic," Larry Broderick would explain in an article in the *Los Angeles Times Magazine* about the murders.

"I knew Dan and I had very similar upbringings, with Catholic education all the way through," Betty said during an interview on the "Oprah Winfrey" show after her trial.

"We were both from large Catholic families," she pointed out.

"Neither sets of our parents have divorced, and we had a lot in common. We had common goals. I wanted a large Catholic family and he wanted to be very successful, and we hit it off."

Betty claimed that Dan pursued her furiously—"the guy asked me to marry him every day for three years" she said in the *Los Angeles Times Magazine* in March 1990. At her trial, she explained further:

> "As soon as I started going out with him, he wanted to get married. I said I wasn't thinking about marriage, I had to get a degree. I was only in my second year. He said I could do both, marry him and finish my college degree. I wanted to do it one at a time. I thought each thing was rather a full-time job."

They dated while Betty pressed to get her teaching degree. She had also been raised with discipline, as well as comforts, and she worked at part-time jobs throughout school for spending money.

"He only had school, tuition money," she testified. "I had a car and disposable income and it was my turf. He'd never been to New York before."

Betty introduced Dan to her friends and took him to her favorite places and restaurants. She made most of the social plans when they went out, but after an acrimonious exchange on one of their first dates, an incident that set the tone for the next twenty years, she always checked with Dan.

"Early on, we were in my car," she recalled. "We were driving to meet my friends, and he pulled over and turned off the key and said, 'Let's get this straight, you don't tell me what we're going to do, ever.' I said, 'Sorry, no big deal. What do you want to do?' And he said, 'I don't have anything to do; just don't tell me what to do.'"

Betty accepted the stricture and recognized no omen for the future. Her dream included a take-charge man, one who knew what he wanted and was willing to do what was necessary to get that. If anything, that early confrontation confirmed her interest in Dan as the kind of man she wanted.

Despite her part-time job and active social life, Betty completed her college credits early, graduating in January 1969. She found work teaching third grade in a suburban Westchester elementary school, and immediately began planning her April wedding. Twenty years later she was still proud of being the first in her college class to marry.

It was a huge, formal affair at the Immaculate Conception Church near her parents' Bronxville home. The bride wore white. Betty's mother assumed the bridegroom would dress formally, but Dan, already displaying signs of a budding dandyism, refused to wear a rented outfit to his own wedding. He appeared in a double-breasted blue pinstripe suit and a flowered tie.

The wedding portrait of the couple on that day pictures an earnest-looking Dan, hair slicked down, sideburns that don't quite reach the bottom of his ears. It was the height of the sixties era of restless rebellion, but only those sideburns distinguish this wedding picture from those of happy couples twenty or twenty-five years earlier. Betty looks as happy as all brides, somewhat smug and pleased with herself.

By her account, that didn't last long.

They honeymooned in a private home on the Caribbean island of St. Thomas, but even that idyllic period developed some dark spots in the romantic fantasy of marriage Betty had built. She told Amy Wallace that Dan "let the maids go," expecting her to "cook and clean" while he studied for his medical school exams.

"When I was brought into the Broderick family," Betty testified, "Larry Broderick said to me, 'Now you're a yuck!' And I said, 'What's a yuck?' He said, 'It's too low to kick and too wet to step on.' That's what they called their sisters, the yucks."

Back in New York, the newlyweds moved into Dan's single dormitory room at Cornell, along with all their wedding gifts. Betty's mother was still angry over her new son-in-law's choice of appropriate wedding attire and refused to store the gifts for the couple. The tiny room adjoined a bathroom they shared with another student who lived in his own small room.

There were other, less immediately obvious, changes, as well. Betty recalled them for the jury:

"A dating relationship is very different from marriage. During dating, I had my own money, my own car. I lived with my parents, but I had some freedom. Afterward, he was in charge of everything. I moved in with him and he took charge of the bank books and my paychecks, and I more or less had to do what he said."

The shining dream of love and marriage was already turning murky. In a matter of weeks Betty was talking about getting a divorce. Dan Broderick, too, soon wanted out. According to an old friend of his, Brian Monaghan, only two weeks after the wedding Dan was crying on a bus in New York City, "aware he had made a terrible and tragic mistake."

In 1988 Dan Broderick also mentioned the early problems in his marriage when he talked to reporters for the *San Diego Reader*, a weekly paper. The original article, about the bitter Broderick divorce, was never printed, but a long article based on those interviews appeared after Dan was killed. He remembered clearly Betty's first threat to end their marriage:

> I swear to God! I couldn't believe it. I was 24 years old. She was upset with me. She would never tell me [why]. She would say, "If you don't know what I'm upset about, then you've got a real problem. I don't want to talk about it. I want to be divorced."

But Betty was expecting a baby. All those years in parochial schools had not included any information on birth control, and she had relied on Dan's medical knowledge. She was pregnant within a month of the ceremony, although she didn't realize it at first.

"After we were married, I got sick right away," she recalled. "I thought it was the flu or something because I kept throwing up and throwing up. I felt terrible, but I kept going to work. I thought I'd get over it. I found out I was pregnant."

When school let out for the summer, she sold nurses' uniforms in a store near the medical school/hospital complex in upper Manhattan. In September, Betty went back to her third-grade class. She was five months pregnant, but Dan was a fourth-year student, and her paycheck from teaching was their only source of spending money.

"I worked every single day," Betty said in court, "until literally the day she was born. January twenty-fourth, 1970, nine months after we got married. It was a Friday, and I taught school that day. Then I went home and had Kim. I did report cards in the hospital over the weekend and didn't go to work on Monday."

The busy young mother hadn't had the time to buy baby clothes or furniture. Kimberly Curtin Broderick slept in a dresser drawer for a crib for a few months, and she was dressed in the Saks Fifth Avenue layette sent by her grandmother Bisceglia, finally forgiving Dan's sartorial lapse with the arrival of a grandchild.

The Brodericks still needed money, but Betty didn't want to leave her infant with a stranger. She found herself a job as a babysitter for another busy young couple in the university complex where they lived.

"In the next building over, there was a woman who was in law school full time," Betty remembered. "The man was a research fellow. They had an eight-month-old daughter. I minded her as a full-time job. I did other babysitting at night. Dan wasn't home, he was studying."

Betty also tried selling Avon and Tupperware door-to-door in the dorm—"none of us lived in a place big enough to have a party"—and took odd jobs whenever she could. Dan, too, had a couple of part-time jobs. Betty remembered that he drove a cab briefly and worked nights for a while in a blood lab, but mostly he studied and she brought in their only spending money.

Years later Betty would tell the *San Diego Reader* how her husband "always looked like a million bucks . . . [with] tailored med coats that were double-breasted, with his initials on the cuff." When asked about it, Dan insisted he wore standard-issue medical school student coats with initials on the pocket.

Whatever their differences, graduation was only a few months away. But the four years of medical school are only the first stage of training for doctors; there are still more years ahead for internship, residency, specialization.

Dan had already decided on another path, and Betty followed his lead. She said later that he made all the decisions about their life together without consulting her, and she didn't question them.

He had applied for law school. Medical malpractice was a fast-growing specialty with multimillion-dollar settlements, and Broderick realized that someone with degrees in both medicine and law would have an advantage.

"Dan is very intelligent, very determined," Betty told the *Reader* in the summer of 1988, after their divorce. "When he wants something, he gets it, and he wanted a big house, big cars, big boats. I can't blame a person for that."

Later, she would tell other interviewers: "I'd vote for being rich any day, wouldn't you?"

It was 1970, the height of the Vietnam War, and another three years of postgraduate school must have seemed very appealing to a draft-age man with family responsibilities. Plus he was accepted at Harvard Law School, generally considered the best legal training in the country.

That sparked another battle between the Brodericks. Betty thought Dan ought to go to work and attend law classes at night. Or, if he insisted on going full-time, choose the less expensive University of Virginia.

Harvard meant borrowing even more tuition money on top of his medical school loan, but he had his own reasoning. "He said, 'You can't say no to Harvard' and he was right," Betty would comment nearly twenty years later.

So Dan and Betty, whom he always called Betts, and Kim moved to Somerville, Massachusetts, a working-class community outside of Boston. The young Broderick family lived in a factory district, with a large resident Portuguese population. Shortly after they moved in, their car was stolen, and Betty didn't have her own washing machine. When Dan came home after class and settled in to study, she'd ride the bus to the closest Laundromat with a plastic bag full of dirty diapers.

Even her outings to the park with Kim evoked colorful memories. "The mothers went to work," she told Jeannette De Wyze and Paul Krueger of the *San Diego Reader*. "So the grandmothers were the ones who were in the playground; these real old ladies with no teeth."

The remembered hard times had acquired a softer patina over the years, and her eyes frequently teared up and her voice would crack as she described her early married life on the witness stand. After the trial, in an interview on "Oprah Winfrey," Betty looked back with some pride to those days when she had lived in Boston.

"When I married Dan Broderick, he was a student," she said. "He was not a doctor or a lawyer, and we were very much in love and we worked very hard, both of us so hard, day and night, to achieve our common goals."

The women's movement was well under way, but Betty never wanted to be anything but a loyal, supportive wife. She put up with the restricted budget and the hard work and the long hours he spent going to school. When she went into labor in 1971 with their second daughter and Dan told her "he was working on an important law school paper and she should drive herself to the hospital," she understood, or so she said in an article about the case that appeared in the September 1991 issue of *Mirabella* magazine.

In the period from 1968 to 1973, when college campuses throughout the country were in turmoil, the Brodericks seem to have passed through four schools untouched by the confusion around them. While many in their generation questioned middle-class morals and motives, Dan and Betty swallowed whole the promise of upward mobility and the good life. In the middle of the sexual revolution, they were having babies.

When other students staged sit-ins and protest marches, the young Brodericks pursued their joint dream of material wealth and success with single-minded purpose; he sitting for long hours in libraries and she sitting in other people's homes, taking care of their children. It was ironic that they missed the generational attitudes in college, because their later lives would often be compared to other pop icons, on movie and television screens.

"Being a supermom was the only thing I ever wanted to be in life," Betty told the "Oprah Winfrey" audience years later. "I did not feel any urge to go out in the world and be successful in business or anything."

Betty may have loved being a wife and mother even while living in student housing without money, but the problems didn't completely disappear and the arguments with Dan were a recurring theme.

It wasn't until after her divorce that she talked about feeling trapped, and in 1988 told the two reporters for the *San Diego Reader*: "Looking back, I think I was the stupidest person in the whole world. But see, then I thought, 'Oh, he works so hard. He's under so much pressure.' And I was happy with my babies."

Broderick, too, recalled Betty's dissatisfaction with the realities of their life together in those early years. In the 1988 interview for the same *Reader* article, he was quoted as saying: "On a regular basis, she expressed extreme unhappiness with me, and my dedication to my work, and my profession, and my attitude toward her and our children."

Dan frequently studied late and sometimes went out drinking afterward with his classmates. He'd come home drunk and playful, dropping to the floor, crawling around imitating an alligator. That's what Betty told a reporter for the March 1991 *Ladies Home Journal*.

She ignored his quirks because "I was taught that love is putting the other person first and making the other person happier than you are, and I did." Before Dan graduated from Harvard, Betty had a third child, a little boy who died two days after he was born.

Then came the day in June when Dan received his degree and could begin earning a living. He had interned the previous summer in Los Angeles and had interviewed with a prestigious San Diego partnership: Gray, Cary, Ames & Frye. One of the city's oldest and most powerful law firms, he accepted the associate job they offered him.

Finally, the long years of graduate school were paying off. Dan would be earning good money and Betty could get a house of her own. They seemed on their way to a life even richer and more comfortable than their childhoods had been. And like most young marrieds, they considered "happily ever after" their birthright.

The Brodericks packed up their daughters, and Dan's medical and legal books and, along with millions of other Americans before and after them, followed the advice of Horace Greeley. The young couple left the loving support of their families and set out to find their own pot of gold at the end of the rainbow and their own interpretation of the American dream in southern California.

4

WILL SUCCESS SPOIL DAN BRODERICK?

THE OLDEST CITY IN THE STATE, SITTING ON A NATURAL HARBOR AND blessed with perfect weather, according to its residents, San Diego seems to be populated with all of the most flamboyant aspects of California's cowboy-biker-surfer mentality, toughened further by the military, represented by active and retired sailors, pilots, Coast Guard, and Marines.

Brash, bright, ambitious, Dan Broderick fit right in.

The Brodericks arrived as San Diego was undergoing an enormous boom. Surrounded by several major military bases and fueled by the Vietnam War, the local economy was expanding briskly. New companies involved in the rapidly growing computer technology, as well as the older defense-related firms, were springing up everywhere.

It was a time made to order for a brilliant young attorney carrying all the built-in arrogance of the medical and legal professions. San Diego offered a perfect location for a hardworking man and his young family. Residents of the California city were used to new arrivals who made themselves at home and quickly became active players in the community's power structure.

For the first couple of years, the Broderick family lived in a rented house in Clairemont. Dan was earning money, finally, but he had large debts for all those years of school, so Betty still didn't have her own washing machine. Their social life centered on Dan's work and the relationships that developed there.

"Gray, Cary ended up being the end-all and the be-all of our lives," she told the *San Diego Reader*. "All of my friends were wives and children of attorneys. Every single one." Parties and social events fostered the firm's closeness, and the Brodericks participated as much as anyone else. Mingling and partygoing were necessary to get ahead in the law firm, and Dan was determined to be a success, financially, socially, and professionally.

"It was just a very old-fashioned kind of imbalanced marriage," Betty told the "Oprah Winfrey" audience after her trials. "I let it be like that. He wanted to be in power and in control. He wanted to be the king of his castle. That's fine with me . . . He handled everything, and that's what he wanted, and it was my job to make him happy, so I didn't fight that, ever."

Dan had the huge student loans to pay off, and Betty continued to take part-time jobs to help the family finances. A fire at the rented house in which they were living brought an insurance settlement that provided them with the cash for a down payment. Dan bought his first house in the Coral Reef section of La Jolla, one of the golden communities of the Golden State.

Site of the Scripps Institute and Clinic, the University of California in San Diego, and several major museums, La Jolla attracts family-oriented professors and professionals. The population of nearly 30,000 includes a large percentage of doctors, lawyers, and engineers. The well-educated, well-connected residents tend to be slightly more liberal than the more military-oriented San Diego voters to the south.

Private country clubs control large chunks of La Jolla real estate, other big parcels belong to the nonprofit institutions, and much of what's left is too steep to build on. Homes in La Jolla are expensive. The most exorbitant are those nearest the ocean, but even the subdivisions on the western side of the mountain carry price tags of six figures.

Described as a tract house, the home Dan bought had the ubiquitous tile roof of southern California. A three-car garage and its drive-way took up most of the frontage, and a deck on the garage roof opened onto the second-story living area.

California subdivisions don't have the broad lawns and picture win-dows of midwestern suburbs. On the mountainous slopes of the highly populated coastal region, less than half the land will support construction. As many houses as possible are squeezed onto the sites that can be used.

The homes in the southern half of the Golden State are on narrow lots with overhanging roofs above narrow windows, to cut the glare of the constant sun. Many are surrounded by hedges and fences, partly for privacy in a climate where backyard patios become an extra room, and partly for safety—to keep the neighbors' kids out of the swim-ming pool.

Despite the physical proximity of the houses, neighbors are often strangers, unless the children are classmates. Families are usually far away, and the high-paying jobs that bring young couples to the golden west depend on the appearance of normalcy. Denying prob-lems is part of the game, and the Brodericks played along with every-one else.

It was 1976 when the Brodericks moved to the five-bedroom home on the southwest side of Mt. Soledad, the mountain that overshadows the center of La Jolla. Betty finally got her own washer and dryer. It would be another few years before the house was completely fur-nished.

There had been a couple more pregnancies ending in miscarriages, but in 1976 Betty gave birth to Daniel T. Broderick IV. After Danny was born, she went back to work as a night hostess and cashier at a nearby Black Angus restaurant, according to the *San Diego Reader*.

Despite the new baby, there were enough obvious strains in the marriage by then for Betty to insist that Dan join her on a Marriage Encounter Weekend sponsored by the church. A product of parochial schools and a strict religious upbringing, Dan was now highly critical of the doctrines of the Catholic faith, but he agreed to her demand. One of the exercises in the workshop was for each participant to write letters to his or her partner.

31

At her first trial, Betty testified that Dan's letter acknowledged "he wasn't the kind of husband he should be," but he had explained that he wanted to provide her with a big house and trips to Europe. He was "almost there. If I would just give him a little more time."

"He said that what he needed in life was to meet financial goals that he set for himself way, way back," she recalled. "When we got there, it was all going to be rosy and it was going to pay off and be wonderful."

Betty's letter, introduced as evidence at the trial, was a cry for recognition:

> You're cold . . . you never have time for me . . . you're not affectionate . . . I feel like I'm living in a bad Del Mar fog or snowstorm or speeding along, not seeing what is ahead, but anticipating a terrible thing . . . We need a sofa so you and I can be physically close in the evenings and share the day's events and feelings.

The reality wasn't matching Betty's dreams, fed on years of television make-believe and movies with happy endings. She had the golden-haired kids and a big house in the suburbs, but she didn't have any furniture, and her husband was never there. The bright dreams of togetherness had tarnished with the drudgery of day-to-day living in two separate worlds, hers with children and school and his at the office.

Instead of the sofa Betty wanted so desperately, Dan Broderick threw himself into his work. He would bring his case files home and fall asleep with the folders on his chest. Longtime friend Brian Forbes, in an article in the March 1991 *Ladies Home Journal*, remembered that even on vacation Dan would be working at the pool: "He'd have a lapful of cases and a highlighter pen. He'd be taking full part in the conversation, but he'd be working at the same time."

Dan's growing success and status also rankled Betty a bit, and when she looked back nearly twenty years later, she saw a reversal of their respective positions in only a few short years. During the worst days after their divorce, she wrote an account of her marriage which she titled "What's a Nice Girl to Do? A Story of White Collar Domestic Violence in America."

The move to California had left her isolated from supportive friends and family back East. She stayed home all day with her small children while her husband blossomed: "Dan went from being a student on his own, with no possessions, no savings, no connections or contacts, to being an M.D./J.D., who had many, many contacts."

Maybe she had no ambition for a high-powered career, but life as supermom wasn't turning out to be exactly what Betty had expected, either. Like so many other women who stay home with children, the larger world ignored her responsibilities and importance, seeing her only in relation to Dan. Her identity was now enmeshed with her husband's, and any recognition she received came from his reflected glory.

Dan moved quickly through the powerful and prestigious law firm, with a combination of hard work, politicking, and skill. Brian Monaghan, a rival attorney who became Dan Broderick's close friend, told an interviewer for the *Los Angeles Times*: "He had an incredible force that stemmed from personal integrity. It was really unusual."

But, according to the *San Diego Reader*, another legal foe had a far different view of Broderick in 1988. The unnamed attorney was less than admiring: "Anybody who's had Dan Broderick on the other side thinks he's a royal jerk . . . He's so difficult to deal with. He's the coldest man you'll ever meet, unless he wants something from you."

Betty remembered Dan bragging that his favorite negotiating posture in a law suit was "sitting on the other guy's chest." He played to win, whether in a court of law or during the regular Saturday morning softball games with other attorneys.

By 1978 Dan was becoming well-known in San Diego as a medical malpractice specialist, and he left Gray, Cary to open his own office. That meant another loan and even longer hours of work and meetings. Still, by refinancing their mortgage, the financial situation had eased enough for the Brodericks to put a swimming pool in the backyard on Coral Reef.

"That's a luxury, right?" Betty asked an interviewer rhetorically.

Dan wrote the checks and handled the family finances and paid the bills, so Betty wasn't sure when he began really making money, but she figured the backyard swimming pool was the first sign of a more comfortable life. That was also when Maria Montes began working for her full-time, doing the housework.

The youngest Broderick child was born in 1979 and he was named after Dan's hero, Rhett Butler, from *Gone With the Wind*. (Dan liked the movie so much, he kept a photo of Clark Gable in costume above his desk. The irreverent Southern gun-runner seemed an odd choice for an attorney raised north of the Mason-Dixon line, but Broderick apparently focused on the more romantic aspects of the character.)

Betty did get pregnant one more time, her ninth in ten years. Warned that her varicose veins and other complications endangered her life, she decided to have an abortion and the surgery that would ensure she would not be pregnant again.

"The sacrifices that I had to put in were doing without my husband while he worked fourteen- or fifteen-hour days and while he social-ized after work and on weekends and he taught courses to other lawyers," Betty said on "Oprah Winfrey."

"All of this was in the name of building his profession, building his name, and I had to do without my husband a lot . . . Dan was very ambitious, and that's what I did. I was a single parent to my children. He was never there. He didn't have time for me or the children."

Instead, Dan put in time at the San Diego Bar Association, serving on committees, attending meetings, lecturing on his specialty to other lawyers and making himself well-known and well-liked among the powers that be in the local legal community. Proud of his Irish back-ground, he also joined the Friendly Sons of St. Patrick, and acquired another round of meetings to attend and committees to head.

Betty spent her time involved with her children. She volunteered at the parochial schools the girls now attended and she served as cookie chairman of the Girl Scouts. On special occasions she went all out.

"My whole life was having traditions for the family on holidays and birthdays," she explained to the jury. "I had lots of decorations and special dishes for each time of the year, Halloween and Easter and Christmas and Thanksgiving and birthdays. It was a real big thing."

Dan's hard work and long hours were finally paying off. He began winning his own multimillion-dollar settlements, and his one-man operation didn't require a lot of overhead. He didn't even have a full-time secretary, preferring to share one with other lawyers.

The beginning of the eighties finally brought real wealth to the Brodericks. They could afford to be true southern Californians, and they joined two country clubs, the Fairbanks Ranch and the La Jolla. The latter has holdings so large, its location is designated on maps of the area. Dan and Betty also became members at the Warner Springs Ranch, a local resort long popular with the San Diego social set.

He finally took Betty to Europe and on cruises to the Caribbean islands. He is reported to have invested in property near Del Mar, another hot spot on the California coast, best known for the racetrack Bing Crosby and his cronies built there in the heyday of Hollywood.

Dan loved to ski, and bought a vacation condominium in Colorado. He got the powerboat he wanted. They entertained regularly, and started collecting imported wines for their cellar. The girls were enrolled in the Bishop's School in La Jolla, and when the boys were old enough, they attended the Francis W. Parker School, both expensive, respected private schools.

"Each child had music lessons," Betty explained on the Winfrey show. "Each child had some sort of sport. I took them all on summer vacations when Dan would never go with us because I do real children things and he . . . didn't like a lot of noise and confusion, and that's what four children are, and I loved it."

Oprah thought it all sounded like "Leave It to Beaver," the TV sitcom of the sixties, and Betty agreed: "Dan went out and slew the dragons and provided for us, and I was home and hearth and children, and supported my husband emotionally and through the good times and the bad."

Betty became active in several charity organizations and hired au pair girls to help with the children. She still volunteered at the schools and took on parental duties like den mother and soccer coach. Kim remembered that "she had a lot of friends."

Dan began really indulging his taste for fashion, ordering custom-made suits. Perhaps in emulation of his swashbuckling fictional idol, he even bought a cape and top hat for formal occasions, wearing it to the Bar Association's annual Blackstone Ball.

Betty still didn't have her own checking account, but she did have credit cards. She, too, liked designer clothes for her charity luncheons and balls. She began to gratify her taste for expensive jewelry as well.

They entertained at home as well as making the legal social scene. For a while Betty had guests for dinner every Sunday night. Dan gave her as much as five thousand dollars a month to cover household expenses and the needs of the children. They were an attractive couple, well-dressed and interesting, and they worked at it as a team.

The society columnist for the local paper, Burl Stiff, recalled the swath the Brodericks cut in those days for the *Los Angeles Times Magazine:* "They both were almost central casting for early yuppie. He always looked straight from Polo. She always had very pretty clothes—Oscar de la Renta and the like."

By 1982 Betty told the *Reader*, "My budget was absolutely unlimited." She could finally furnish the house the way she wanted, although Dan was already talking about buying a bigger place.

The new wealth provided a more comfortable lifestyle, but the problems, what Dan later called "basic incompatibility," remained. He continued to work late and go out drinking with friends. He was stopped several times and received a couple of tickets for drunk driving.

Betty, who rarely drank heavily, didn't like most of Dan's drinking buddies. She resented his apparent preference for their company in the bars of downtown San Diego to being at home with her and the children.

"I'd get very upset with him for never coming home," Betty remarked during an interview with Kathleen Neumeyer for the *Ladies Home Journal* article. "I'd cry all the time, but I'd get over it. I totally loved the guy."

Betty expanded her complaints to ABC's Tom Jarriel in an interview for "20/20" during her second trial: "I was the soccer coach and the Boy Scout leader . . . I was a real hands-on, in-the-mud-with-the-kids mom. Dan was never there. He was too busy."

Kim, the oldest of the four Broderick children, recalled the battles between her parents. Betty threw a stereo at Dan when he returned after taking the kids out for pizza with another lawyer.

"She would scratch him or stick her fingernails in his arms," Kim testified. She remembered that her mother would lock her husband out when she was angry, and Dan Broderick would come to his eldest daughter's window and whisper for her to open the door for him.

Dan also had a temper. He "hated" dogs, according to his daughter Lee, and at least once is reported to have kicked the family pet. He "would break things that would frustrate him," like the lawn mower. At other times he broke an aquarium and ripped a door off its hinge. Betty remembered that he threw one door out of a window in a rage.

When Dan came home in a bad mood, Betty would warn the kids to stay quiet and out of his way. "Nobody would want to disobey him or make him mad when he was home from work," Lee said.

Maria Montes, the longtime family maid, also testified that the children, especially the younger boys, were often "frightened and silent" around their father. Dan wouldn't let them jump or play, Montes said through an interpreter. "He would just scream and say 'sit down' and they would have to sit down."

Although she remembered some bad moments, Lee had a completely different version of Broderick family life than her sister's. "I thought we had a really happy family," the younger girl testified. She rarely remembered seeing her mother cry, saying Betty "would hold back her tears if she was upset" when any of the children were around.

Lee didn't remember many arguments between her parents. "If they were fighting, it wasn't in front of us," she recalled. "They'd go into their bedroom and lock the door and fight in there. My parents didn't fight that much."

Kim admitted that her mother's anger was usually spread throughout the family, not directed just at Dan. Betty would throw frozen food at the kids when she was mad at them, and sometimes hit the children when they did something wrong.

Once, Kim recalled, her sister Lee was "being bratty" and taunting their mother, saying the spanking didn't hurt. Betty chased her with a fly swatter, and the wire left welts on the girl's legs.

Sometimes the Brodericks would have plans to go out for the evening; Betty would be dressed and ready to go, and at the last minute change her mind. Dan usually went off without her on those nights. In the 1988 interview with the *San Diego Reader*, he admitted, "I was far from the kind of good, loving husband I could have been."

Kathy Broderick, married to Dan's brother Larry at the time, also remembered arguments between Betty and Dan. In an October 21, 1991 *People* magazine that appeared during Betty's second trial, Kathy claimed that Betty would make fun of Dan, "calling him fag to his face."

Betty was usually the one who talked about a divorce. Following that first threat after their honeymoon, she would repeat it whenever she was angry. "Hundreds, I mean hundreds of times," Dan remembered in 1988.

Kim, too, recalled her mother's threats to move out. Betty would tell the children she was divorcing their father, then ask them which parent they wanted to live with. Kim's choice was Dan, but he would deny there was going to be a divorce.

Still, it all sounds like a fairly typical American family. Only on TV sitcoms do adults live together without arguments. Only in the movies does life go on "happily ever after." But for most couples, at least until the sixties, when the divorce rate hit fifty percent, it did go on.

Betty Broderick, a devout Catholic married to a man with a parochial school education, expected her marriage to last her lifetime. As she told the "Oprah Winfrey" audience: "I took those marriage vows and I believe he did at the time, too, believing that we'd be together and we'd work together and we'd get through everything and we'd build a life for ourselves and our children."

Fourteen years after that formal wedding at the Immaculate Conception Church in Bronxville, New York, she learned that she had been wrong.

5

Fourteen-Year Itch

"Isn't she beautiful?"

Betty Broderick overheard the comment her husband made to another man at a cocktail party late in 1982 or early the next year, she recalled on the witness stand. Although many of her friends were attractive women, she had never before heard Dan express such open admiration for any of them.

She wondered who had caught his attention like that. When she asked him later, he told her that he had been talking about the receptionist on the floor of his office building in downtown San Diego.

"That was my first clue that Linda Kolkena existed," Betty would tell the "Oprah Winfrey" show audience nine years later.

Like many in San Diego's legal community, Dan had located his one-man office near the courts in the heart of the downtown business district. He kept his overhead low by using a free-lance typist, making his own appointments, and using the floor receptionist to screen calls for the first couple of years. He did all the legal research on his cases himself and filed the motions and briefs in court. By 1983, when his income was skyrocketing, so was his workload. Betty thought that he could now afford to hire help, allowing him more free time with the family at home.

Later, Betty would say, "Nineteen eighty-three was like an axe through my life."

That spring, the Brodericks went to Europe again. They had company—another couple who traveled as Dan's guests—and they stayed in the most expensive hotels, but the trip was no pleasure for Betty.

"Dan was very tense and just not himself on a vacation," she recalled during the Winfrey show. But they had been married for fourteen years, they had four children, things were going well financially, and "we had total trust in one another, as we should have . . ."

During the summer, Betty took the four kids away for a camping trip through the West. Dan stayed home because he had too much work to do and didn't like camping anyway; ski vacations were the only kind he took with the children. The family was gone more than a month. Dan never seemed to be home when Betty and the kids called while they were away to say hello.

"He didn't seem happy to see us," Betty recalled of the family's return to San Diego. "I hadn't been home one minute when I knew something was wrong."

The next day she found out what. As they drove to a wedding a few miles up the coast, Dan Broderick told his wife that he was unhappy with his life.

"He thought our house was tacky, he thought our friends were boring," Betty testified. And he wasn't too pleased with her, either.

"He said I was old, fat, ugly, boring, and stupid," Betty recalled at her trials.

The five adjectives seemed to take on a mantralike quality in her interviews and testimony—"old, fat, ugly, boring, and stupid."

Betty used the quintet of words like a lash whenever her anger at Dan Broderick flagged in the days and years ahead. Every time she repeated them, she seemed to be hearing them for the first time, and the fury would build in her voice as she pronounced each word in the damning list.

Dan Broderick, thin and studious in his youth, driven and ambitious in the early years of his marriage, was coming into his own with middle age. Betty commented acidly to the *San Diego Reader* journalists in the summer of 1988 that "most men his age are overweight and balding, but Dan has gained some weight and it looks great."

Apparently the reporters agreed the attorney was a late bloomer. They described him as "impeccably tailored . . . of striking good looks," and commented that at forty-four he could have easily passed for someone ten years younger.

At the time, Betty blamed Dan's moodiness on hard work and she was delighted when he came home that September and announced that he had finally hired an office assistant.

"I was very, very happy about that," she explained on the witness stand. "I thought it would be a release valve and would mean more time for us . . . He had been so grouchy and under so much pressure . . ."

Then she learned that Dan's new assistant was Linda Kolkena. Betty had been aware of the tall, attractive blonde ever since the cocktail party, when she overheard Dan's comment about the receptionist's looks. Helpful friends had called to report whenever Dan "was seen out to lunch and out to drinks at different places downtown" with the twenty-two-year-old former stewardess.

Like the Brodericks, Linda was the product of a strict Catholic upbringing. Her parents were Dutch, arriving in the United States in 1955 after growing up during the Nazi occupation of their native country. They settled in Salt Lake City, where Arnold Kolkena found work on a loading dock, a job he would keep for the next thirty-seven years.

The youngest of four children, Linda was eleven when her mother —a cheerful, optimistic woman—died after a long battle with breast cancer in 1972. Two weeks after the funeral, on Linda's twelfth birthday, the family, in the midst of its grief, forgot the young girl's special day. Much later Linda would tell her sister Margaret that she "felt abandoned" that year.

Despite the tragedy of her mother's death, their childhood, Margaret said, sounded "too good to be true." She described a warm, close-knit family governed by "a strong work ethic" and old-world values. She remembered sitting around the dining room table playing geography games with her father, who looked to his children, not sports or hobbies, for leisure.

"I remember my father saying he liked a job he could leave at the end of the day," Margaret recalled.

Linda started working as a teenager, babysitting for neighbors in Mormon, family-oriented Salt Lake City. Margaret remembered that her sister often went straight from school to help a woman down the block who had seven children. Like Betty Broderick, Linda Kolkena loved children and hoped for a large family.

After high school she became a flight attendant for Delta Air Lines, but left under something of a cloud.

(Betty Broderick's defense team learned that Linda had been asked to leave the airline after she used obscene language to another stewardess on a flight where Kolkena was flying as a passenger. According to the defense investigators, Linda indulged in heavy petting with a male passenger after getting drunk on the flight and she cursed when reprimanded. Asked to explain the incident to a supervisor, Linda reportedly said that she used vulgar language all the time and so it didn't seem inappropriate to her.)

Kolkena came to southern California sometime in 1982, apparently trailing a boyfriend. That relationship ended shortly after she took the job as a receptionist that brought her into Dan Broderick's orbit, according to another one of Linda's beaus. Steve Kelley is an editorial cartoonist for the *San Diego Union* and was interviewed by Kathleen Neumeyer in the March 1991 *Ladies Home Journal* article.

Kelley was dating Linda himself, and he recalled that "she talked all the time about her boss, what an incredible guy he was." The cartoonist, apparently a bit jealous, probed further, but he said that Linda had denied she was involved with Dan. Kelley explained he grew suspicious when he saw her spacious office and learned that she was earning a salary of $30,000 as an assistant in a one-man law firm although she had no legal training.

"She wasn't a paralegal," Betty pointed out in court. "She wasn't a lawyer. She wasn't even a secretary; she couldn't type. He needed a lot of help, and I couldn't see that she was the person to help him."

Betty had tried to ignore the earlier clues, like the unfamiliar bathing suits Maria Montes had reported finding around the swimming pool while the family was camping the past summer. But the latest move was a humiliating and public slap in the face. She confronted her husband:

"I said it's bad enough you're having an affair with this person, but now you're going to pay her to be with you twelve to fourteen hours a day while I'm home alone with the kids. I gave him a month to get rid of the girl, October first. I was being nice, stupidly . . . I said get rid of her by October first or get out of my house."

Dan told Betty she was "crazy . . . delusional . . . imagining things." He denied having an affair, denied any involvement with Linda Kolkena except as his office assistant, and, in an ominous note for the future, informed Betty that "if there was anything going on I didn't like, I could get out of the house, because it was his house."

Betty's ultimatum passed and nothing happened. Linda continued to work in the office at 401 West A Street. And in the Broderick house on Coral Reef, the tensions grew. Now there were even more nights when Dan didn't come home until very late. Or he'd leave again after dinner.

"We had talks about his being unhappy," Betty remembered on the witness stand. "I'd say I don't know what you're talking about. You have four healthy kids, a beautiful home, you're doing well in business, we're healthy. What else is there in life? I don't understand why you're all of a sudden so unhappy."

Betty liked the status quo, but Dan was looking toward the future. He was aiming for leadership, starting with the Bar Association. He knew he had to make a splash, and he described his plans to Betty.

"He said he wanted a lot of changes, major changes," she went on. "He wanted a new house, a mansion. He wanted us to live a much more glamorous lifestyle. He was a real grouch around me and the kids, from my perspective. He had me walking on eggshells trying to please him."

When Dan came home one night with a red Corvette, Betty bought books on male mid-life crisis. They didn't help.

On her thirty-sixth birthday, November 7, Dan didn't come home in time for dinner, and Betty was distraught. It wasn't easy, but she tried to pretend there was nothing wrong. She'd had years to practice distracting the children's attention from their father's absence.

"I covered up like I always did, and the kids and I had dinner and a party," she recalled in tearful, emotional testimony. "I put the kids to bed . . . and then I slit my wrists and swallowed every pill I could find in the house."

Unwilling to stay in the bedroom she shared with Dan, she lay down on the bed in a spare bedroom and passed out. Her next memory is of the following morning, and Dan shaking her awake. She never found out if he came home the night before and didn't notice that he slept alone in their bed until he woke up, or if he came looking for her when he got in the next morning and discovered the master bedroom empty.

The cuts on her wrist were superficial and her husband used his medical training to bandage them. She hadn't taken enough pills to do more than put her to sleep and make her groggy the next day.

Betty testified that Dan cried when he realized what she had done, and he told her the kids couldn't manage without her. He even apologized for making her feel bad, but insisted again that "nothing was going on with Linda."

Instead, he suggested that she "should get some help," Betty recalled, "that I was having a mental breakdown, that I needed help because I was imagining all these things."

Feeling insecure and unsure of her own judgments, she turned to her friends for help. One suggested that she take control of the situation by going to the law office on West A Street and making herself known. It sounded like a good idea. Two weeks later, on Dan's thirty-ninth birthday, Betty, who so loved to make special celebrations, decided to follow the advice.

At his request, she had baked a home-made chocolate cake and prepared a roast beef for the family dinner. Then Betty Broderick put on her makeup, picked up a bottle of champagne and an ice bucket, and late in the afternoon headed for her husband's office in downtown San Diego to surprise him. She expected to toast his birthday while they watched the sunset together before returning home.

When she arrived at West A Street, Betty discovered she was too late. The office was already festooned with birthday decorations and there were remnants of a chocolate mousse cake in the refrigerator. She hadn't even known he had a refrigerator in the office, or a stereo system. Betty said she also found a half-empty bottle of wine and two wineglasses from her wedding crystal. But she didn't find Dan, or Linda.

The receptionist who had Linda's former job told her the pair had left before lunch and hadn't returned. Betty decided to wait. She walked around, noticing the brass nameplate on Linda's door and the view from the floor-to-ceiling windows in her office.

Betty also saw the picture on the wall of a youthful Dan, age twenty-two. Taken before their marriage, it was apparently a gift to his legal assistant. Steve Kelley had spotted the photograph, too, describing in the *Ladies Home Journal* a photo of Dan on horseback "with the horse rearing up. It was like a knight in shining armor."

Betty had a different reaction to the photo. "I said, 'God, what's his picture doing on the wall? This is really tacky,' " she recalled in her testimony.

She watched the sunset alone from Dan's office, waiting for him to return, then drove back to La Jolla in a fury. When she returned to Coral Reef, she stormed into their bedroom, gathered up the custom-made suits from Dan's closet and dropped them in the backyard. As the four children watched, she sprinkled the pile with gasoline and set them afire. Then she dumped black paint on what didn't burn. Everything but the cape and top hat.

Dan arrived at home to find his prized suits a smoldering ruin and Betty waiting for him at the front door with his checkbook. She explained during her testimony that he had once said if he ever left her, all he needed was his red Corvette and the checkbook, and she could keep the children and the family life.

"So he had his Corvette and I handed him his checkbook and I said, 'You're out of here,' " she recalled in court.

"I can't imagine what I could have done, short of shooting him, that would have been a stronger statement than this," she wrote several years after the event in the unpublished account of her marriage.

"Now, if he was innocent and he came home and his nutsy wife had burned his clothes, wild horses couldn't have kept him there, so I mean he was as guilty as anything. I caught him with his pants down," Betty said during an interview with the ABC news program "20/20."

But once again Betty backed down. He offered an explanation. He and Linda had gone to lunch to celebrate his birthday, then spent the afternoon taking depositions, he said. There was no affair, he insisted, Betty was imagining things.

"Before this point in our then long-term marriage, I'd never doubted what he'd told me before," she testified. "If he told me he was at a meeting, he was at a meeting. If he said he was at a deposition, that's where he was."

Kim remembered her father going to the backyard that night and watched as he "picked up the few pieces that weren't burned or ruined, and then they went to bed, like everything was normal."

The only apparent effect of Betty's outrageous gesture was on the finances of the tailor who made Dan's clothes. "He just ordered all new clothes," she recalled in the 1988 *Reader* interview. "His tailor loved me."

Life in the Broderick house continued as before, but the atmosphere was getting very strained. Betty, convinced her husband was going through a mid-life crisis, decided she should take action to make herself more interesting and attractive to him.

"I just tried not to be so 'old, fat, ugly, boring, and stupid,' " she said. "I couldn't do anything about being old. I lost weight. I went down to sickly thin. I didn't think I was boring, but I quit all my society things and tried to stay home and give him more attention . . . I tried to be really perfect for him so he'd have nothing to complain about at all."

She went to a dentist for braces to straighten a crooked tooth, and on Dan's recommendation, went to one of his clients "to get the wrinkles off my face." She let her hair grow longer, the way it was when they first met, and even spoke to a doctor about reversing her earlier surgery so she could have another child.

"If it would make Dan feel younger to have babies around, I would have the operation reversed and have more children," Betty explained on the witness stand. "I was asking, what does she have that we don't have together?"

According to friends, Linda Kolkena could make serious-minded, sober-sided Dan Broderick act silly. He laughed when she recited the instructions she'd memorized as a flight attendant. A happy woman with a bubbly sense of humor, Linda could even get Dan to act out scenes from Peter Sellers movies.

Life with Betty was not as much fun. He continued to work late and to offer excuses. He continually denied any relationship beyond employer and employee with Linda Kolkena, but apparently considered late evenings at the Bar Association together as work. Dan repeated his advice to Betty that she needed professional help because she was imagining things.

Her defense lawyer later claimed to have found a man, the son of a local hotel owner, who made a room available to Dan and Linda for afternoon trysts, but the evidence was not introduced at the trial.

"I had feelings and impressions of what I thought was true," Betty recalled on the witness stand. "He was telling me that was not true. I felt imbalanced . . . All the clues were pointing one way, and he's telling me black is white and white is black. I was feeling a little off-balance. I'd never felt like that before."

Looking back, Betty decided that her husband was just following good legal tactics in the next months. "Dan transformed himself from a husband to a lawyer plotting strategy in his case," she told Amy Wallace of the *Los Angeles Times*.

Like the top-flight litigator he was, Dan Broderick automatically denied any wrongdoing, especially when the accusation involved something as potentially damaging as adultery, which might later be used against him. He may also have been in conflict over the Catholic values imbued in childhood and his adult decisions; that was the opinion of his brother Larry when he tried to explain the years Dan spent with Betty in the *Los Angeles Times* article.

Jack Earley found an even more sinister explanation. He became convinced that Broderick was using the time to transfer community property assets to Larry's Colorado-based investments. The defense attorney also saw evidence that Dan was hoping his contradictory actions would so unbalance Betty she would agree to professional help, preferably in a hospital.

The tensions continued to build, and even the children started to notice the change in Betty's attitude. "In my trying to please Dan Broderick and make things perfect for him," she testified, "I became very tense and short-tempered with the children, and they never knew why."

But they did notice the growing animosity between the two adults they were living with. The frequent arguments—Betty's hysterical scenes, Dan's angry denials—were impossible to ignore even if they didn't know what the battles were about.

Oldest daughter Kim, who was just fourteen that troubled year, told the court that "as far as I could see, Daddy was taking care of us, doing the best he could, and Mom was just ruining everything."

She remembered her father as "nice and really loving and affectionate" when he got drunk, but said her mother would "be mad at him" if he was "out late with his friends."

Lee was less aware of the disputes. On "Oprah Winfrey" she wistfully recalled that "we had a nice house and a nice family and . . . everything just fell apart piece by piece."

In 1984 the Brodericks made another trip to Europe. Steve Kelley, still going out with Linda Kolkena, saw her frequently while they were gone, according to the *Ladies Home Journal* article. He remembered that she was driving Dan's beloved Corvette while he was away, and that long-stemmed red roses arrived on her birthday, although Dan had not yet returned.

Betty continued to believe that her husband was going through a mid-life crisis. "We lived in a community where this is a pretty common problem with men at mid-life, and several of my friends had gone through similar [things]," she explained on the Winfrey show.

There was no discussion about a divorce as they struggled through 1984 together. They talked about buying the larger house that Dan wanted, and began making plans to sell the one on Coral Reef.

Betty was still getting calls from friends, reporting sightings of Dan and Linda together at lunch or dinner in the downtown restaurants the legal community favored. When she confronted him about these incidents, Dan denied again that there was anything going on with Linda.

"He looked me in the eye and lied and lied and lied and lied a billion times," she told a jury.

After years of ambivalence, Dan Broderick had apparently finally rejected the rigid values of his church and childhood. He took on instead the more liberal moral standards of his environment—California and, specifically, San Diego. He changed the rules in their very conventional marriage without telling Betty.

He continued to ridicule her suspicions of what was happening, coming up with excuses, explanations, and rationalizations to counter every accusation she made. For a long time she accepted what he said because she wanted so badly for it to be true. But sooner or later even an ostrich begins to realize that sticking its head in the sand doesn't really get rid of its problem, but only presents a larger, and stationary, target.

"I sort of believed it," Betty said in 1988 to the *San Diego Reader*. "But it got to the point where you had to be blind, stupid, and everything else in order to believe it."

At her second trial she was asked how she felt when she heard Dan's continuous denials in the face of her suspicions.

"It made me feel like a jerk," she replied, sobbing. "Like I was stupid or something. There are no words to describe how you feel when you find your husband is having an affair."

During an inspection prior to putting the Coral Reef house on the market, a crack was discovered in its foundation, an apt symbol for the Broderick homestead. As usual, Dan made the decision to move the family to a rental until repairs could be made. Betty was not consulted. He explained that the house could not be sold until the foundation was fixed.

The Broderick family moved out of Coral Reef and into another five-bedroom house, this one in La Jolla Shores, a community right on the edge of the Pacific Ocean. They lived there together through the round of birthdays in November, then the string of holidays at the end of the year.

On February 28, 1985, Kim remembered her mother getting angry and throwing a bottle of Dom Pérignon champagne at Dan. Betty says her husband just came home that day and announced he "needed more space" and was leaving.

"He literally walked out three months after his fortieth birthday party—with a red Corvette and a twenty-one-year-old," Betty told the pair of reporters from the *San Diego Reader*. "Are we the American joke or not?

"If you weren't my husband, I'd think you were real funny. He's got a scarf around his neck and he wanted those Ray-Ban sunglasses from *Risky Business*. I said, 'You're it! You are the cover of 'Midlife Crisis' magazine. Cool, Dan, cool.' "

Three years later Dan apparently still resented the suggestion his life had been a middle-aged cliché. "She glosses over a lot when she says we were both happy," Dan remarked to the *San Diego Reader* reporters. "She tells my children that we had a blissful, happy, healthy marriage until I went crazy when I was forty. That's just pure fiction! It's a figment of her imagination that's not even close."

Dan moved back into the empty house on Coral Reef although the repairs there were not quite finished. He slept on a mattress on the floor for the first few days. Betty and the children stayed in the rental house, as she tried to figure out what had gone wrong with her marriage.

A life of total togetherness with a loving and supportive husband was a long-forgotten illusion for Betty Broderick by 1984, but the promise of a marriage that lasted a lifetime regardless of the stresses and pressures remained one of her most cherished dreams.

They were Catholics. Marriages were for eternity, and somehow one coped with the hard times and rejoiced in the good. That was what she had been taught as a child, that was what she believed as an adult, and that is what she thought her husband had been committed to.

He had left temporarily. She just had to give him time to adjust to being forty, to get over his mid-life crisis and his middle-aged passion for Linda Kolkena. This was just a phase, something they would be able to laugh about one day together.

But Dan already knew that would never happen. Betty, too, probably understood, even then, that her marriage was over and the future she had expected would never be. Nothing else explains the anger, even rage, that would grow and expand, eventually overwhelming every other emotion. Her fury denuded her maternal instincts and destroyed her personality.

Feeling foolish and betrayed, Betty Broderick became determined not to be taken advantage of again, especially not by Dan. She was not going to sit silently by as the wronged, but hopeful, wife awaiting his pleasure.

6

WAR OF THE BRODERICKS

"FRANKLY MY DEAR, I DON'T GIVE A DAMN."
Betty Broderick swore Dan plagiarized his hero's best-known line. She claimed that he saw his opportunity as he was moving out on the last day of February 1985. When she asked him how she and the children were going to live in the rented house without money or a checking account, Dan responded with the words Margaret Mitchell wrote for Rhett Butler when he walked away from Scarlett.

For six weeks Betty went through the motions of taking care of her four children while she struggled to understand what had happened to her marriage and her life. The reports of Dan and Linda having dinner in downtown restaurants continued, but Dan resolutely denied that his departure had anything to do with another woman. He told Betty that he just "needed space."

Apparently believing she needed more space, too, Betty tried a desperate countermeasure—restricting his freedom by adding the children. Just six weeks after Dan left the family hearth, eldest daughter Kim was the first to arrive on his doorstep.

"It was on Easter," Kim told Amy Wallace of the *Los Angeles Times* five years later. "I asked her to drive my friend home, and she lost it," Kim recalled. "She said, 'Pack your bags.' " Kim sat for hours at the front door waiting for her unsuspecting father to come home and let her in.

Betty remembered the Saturday before Easter as the day when the strain of living with four children by herself became too much and she lost her self-control. "I was overwhelmed and needed help," she testified.

Kim was quarreling with Lee and they were driving her crazy. Betty drove her oldest child to Coral Reef and left her on the doorstep to wait for Dan's return. It was Danny, then nine, that she dropped off the next day, Easter Sunday, even though his older sister remembers the youngster "was really upset."

The lease on the rental was up in June and Betty wanted to move. She said the house was overrun with rats. That's why she sent Lee and Rhett to join Danny and Kim in Coral Reef without a warning to Dan.

Kim remembered the arrival as a nightmare of crying and screaming. Her younger brother did not want to leave his mother, and clung to her, but Betty was adamant, telling all four children: "I'm leaving. Your dad's not going to get away with this . . . Let him try to deal with four kids."

By then fifteen-year-old Kim had some idea of the problems between her parents. She testified that Betty brought up Linda's name frequently and hinted at something more, but didn't openly accuse Dan of having an affair to her children until he moved back to Coral Reef. Kim said she thought her mother's accusation was "crazy," but she asked Dan about it. The young woman remembered that her father had denied any involvement with Linda Kolkena.

While his denials to Betty are perhaps understandable as legal tactics, Dan's lie to Kim seems inexplicable. Perhaps he thought she would testify against him if he told her the truth. Or he may have just been concerned that she would turn against him if she knew Betty's accusation had some merit.

Dan recalled how the children had arrived, one by one, when he talked to the *San Diego Reader* in 1988. "[Betty] would just leave them there with their personal things, their clothes, and wouldn't tell me they were coming, and just drop them there. 'Here. They're yours. You want to be apart from me. Well, see what it's like raising a family by yourself.' "

Now Dan was living with all four children in the house on Coral Reef while Betty was alone in a rented house that she said was over-run with rats. She claimed at one point that the rodents destroyed a closet full of her designer evening gowns. Such living conditions in the house were too dangerous for the children.

"At first, Dad figured that she was going to come take us back," Kim remembered in court. "He had no idea what to do with us, and then, gradually, he got very good at it."

Apparently somewhat indignant at first that he should be responsi-ble for the children, Dan Broderick eventually used their presence as the ultimate weapon against Betty. She had expected the needs of four children to make him aware of her value in his life and presence in his home. Instead, Dan found ways to manage without her alto-gether and without making too many alterations in his own life.

Unable to be home all the time, and uninterested in the minutia of housework, Broderick hired housekeepers and later even a governess to help. He changed some of his habits, bringing his work home at night instead of staying at the office so he could share dinner with the children. He made sure they did their homework. He imposed disci-pline, according to Kim, and sometimes the kids complained about that to their mother.

Betty was living in La Jolla Shores, but she still seemed to spend a lot of time at the Coral Reef house. She bought the kids' favorite snack foods and made sure they got to all of their extracurricular activities after school. She insisted that her appearances were only in response to their complaints about an empty refrigerator and bare cupboards. She seemed to come and go as she pleased.

The unusual arrangement continued for a few months, but in June the Broderick marriage moved into another phase. A family counsel-ing expert would explain at Betty's trial about the growing rage that builds in a spouse whose partner lies about an affair; about the be-trayal of a promise and the distrust that breeds. Betty may have been further infuriated by Dan Broderick's growing ability to cope with four children and a household in her absence.

Whatever the initial spark, beginning that June, Betty erupted periodically in spasms of outlandish and even violent gestures.

"She started on rampages," Dan recalled for the *San Diego Reader*. "Throwing stuff through the windows and breaking mirrors and spray-painting the walls. I mean, unbelievable things."

In papers filed as part of the ongoing divorce actions, Broderick alleged that in June, Betty vandalized his bedroom, destroying an answering machine, smashing a hole in a wall, breaking the mirrors and spraying black paint on a brick wall and fireplace.

In August, Marta Shaver, Dan's housekeeper at the time, remembered Betty coming to the house. Finding a Boston cream pie Linda Kolkena had made for the family on the kitchen counter, Betty smeared it all over Dan's bedroom. The housekeeper, busy in the kitchen, testified that she noticed Betty running from the house, but paid little attention to the woman, who was always in and out. Then she heard Lee screaming. The housekeeper said that she ran upstairs to find "the entire room was devastated."

Dan recalled another invasion by Betty when he was talking to the *Reader* in 1988: "At one time, I had taken the kids to get haircuts, and she was expecting them at a soccer game. I didn't know they were supposed to be at a soccer game.

"I'm not that kind of person that I would take them to get a haircut just to spite her. I came back and there were hundreds, maybe thousands of dollars in damages. I mean, windows broken and chandeliers cracked and stereo smashed. It was unbelievable stuff."

Broderick went to the local police for help, but learned that they were helpless without a court order. Betty's name was on the deed and "she can do whatever she wants," Dan remembered them saying.

The only solution was to put Betty's name on another deed and sell the house that she still considered her home. Dan had wanted to move for a couple of years anyway.

He made the down payment on a $650,000 house Betty selected, one with a view of the ocean on the winding Calle del Cielo, in the area between Torrey Pines Road and the Pacific in La Jolla Shores.

Betty started fixing up the house, adding a pool, poolhouse, and volleyball court for the children. She still expected to be living with her family again.

On September 23 Dan filed for divorce.

Betty insisted he originally wanted to serve her with the divorce papers while she was attending a luncheon for the Bishop's School. She said she had seen a memo detailing the plan to humiliate her at one of La Jolla's most exclusive social events. The memo was never made public. But Betty knew what the future would be like, as she recounted to ABC's Tom Jarriel:

"Dan was a killer attorney. This is where he knew how to win. That's how he made so much money. From the day he filed those first papers . . . he would never talk to me as a person. Everything had to be done in the courtroom, where he was the big gun, the powerhouse, never eyeball-to-eyeball, person-to-person, God forbid, husband to wife."

There had been a warning that the official court move was coming, but Betty, as usual, tried to ignore it. Early that September, Dan came over and told her she would be paying her own bills from then on. He went over her expenses and announced he would give her $9,000 a month for her needs. He also agreed to continue paying her insurance, taxes, and the fees for her social outlets, including the country clubs and charities.

She remembered that conversation but told the reporters from the *San Diego Reader* that the actual divorce petition came as a shock. "I give everyone the benefit of the doubt until they come up and shoot me between the eyes . . . I was real surprised and upset, and I needed a lawyer fast."

Betty knew a lot of attorneys, of course. That was the problem. She knew them through Dan and they were his friends, not hers. She told the *Reader* that she eliminated most of the matrimonial lawyers she had recommended to others because they were too involved with Dan. Dozens more she rejected because she didn't think they were up to the battle with Dan Broderick in court.

He had developed a reputation as a tough litigator. Betty had heard all about his triumphs over the years, especially his favorite story of serving one doctor with notice of a malpractice suit at Christmas Eve church services. Other defendants remembered coming home from vacation to find a notice that Dan Broderick was filing a lawsuit against them, and their house and car were at risk.

"I needed a killer, an intelligent, button-down, smart-ass attorney," Betty said. "In the divorce business there are very few of those." She called some, but she found none willing to take her case. One, Thomas Ashworth, turned her down saying he was going to be appointed to Family Court shortly. He turned up as Dan's attorney until the judgeship came through.

Finally, at the suggestion of San Diego attorney Bonnie Nelson Reading, Betty looked beyond the local legal talent and retained Daniel Jaffe, a Beverly Hills divorce lawyer.

"The day I was to go to L.A. to hire Jaffe, I went to Coral Reef first," Betty testified. "I said, 'Dan, why are you making me do this? I don't want to hire a lawyer. Let's get together and work this out. I don't think I should hire an attorney. It's just a lot of money wasted.' I just didn't want to hire a lawyer."

By then, however, the feelings on both sides were too entrenched and the emotions too raw. The previous Christmas, Betty Broderick had learned the word "cunt" from her friend and neighbor, Gail Forbes. Betty, who had rarely used coarse language before, employed the vulgarity whenever she talked about Linda.

For Dan she reserved the term "fuckhead."

"He was attacking me, overpowering me," Betty explained in her testimony. "The only way I had to fight back was to call him names. Big deal."

Dan's relationship with Linda Kolkena was no longer a secret. She had accompanied him to Colorado for Larry Broderick's annual Oktoberfest party. When Betty found out that Linda had been part of a Broderick family party, she again insisted on seeing Dan. He admitted that she had "been right all along" about the affair.

As a Catholic, Betty expressed outrage that her children were being exposed to the adulterous relationship. When she made her feelings known to Dan, she remembered a confrontation that bordered on violent because "he wanted to take me to a mental institution."

All four children had met Linda. And Lee remembered that Betty wasn't the only one calling names.

Dan and Linda referred to Betty as "fat, disgusting, beastly, the Beast, the Monster, on the rampage, on the warpath," Lee told the court.

Her father refused to have anything to do with her mother, the young woman remembered. He "didn't want to talk to her, he didn't want to see her, he didn't want to hear her voice," Lee said.

Dan's friends said that he tried to work things out with Betty at first, but she would start cursing him and screaming whenever they met. If he tried to drive away, Betty would jump in his car and continue her verbal attacks. Once she nearly broke off the aerial when he tried to leave.

According to those who claimed to know, Dan decided there was no point to seeing her personally any longer. Any further contact would be through attorneys or the court. They were on opposite sides in the adversarial process.

Legally Dan had every right to restrict his contact with Betty, but a history of nearly twenty years and nine pregnancies would seem to call for a larger effort on his part. Psychologists agree the most profound sense of loss comes to a parent at the death of a child, but every grief recalls the previous losses in someone's life. Betty had suffered the loss of five babies before or immediately after birth. Dan's leaving added yet another horrendous loss, this time abandonment. The emotional pain seemed to affect Betty's thinking.

At the time Dan filed for divorce, Judge J. Richard Haden issued standard orders to both parties to avoid harassing each other. When that didn't keep Betty away, Broderick got a temporary restraining order, prohibiting her from coming within a hundred yards of his person or property. Betty refused to accept a judicial decision that didn't let her approach her own children.

"She kept saying, 'This is my house. I can come in whether you like it or not. I don't have to listen to the court order. The court can't keep me out of my own house,'" Dan recalled in 1988.

Broderick controlled Betty's finances and tried to control her actions and language as well. He seemed to think that she shouldn't express her anger to him. Or maybe he didn't think she had any reason to be angry. He explained his reasoning to the *San Diego Reader* in 1988:

> "I wrote her a letter and I said, 'Look, if you don't stop harassing me, I'm going to withhold two hundred dollars for every obscene word you use, five hundred dollars every time you come into my house, and a thousand dollars every time you take the kids away without telling me in advance."

Further enraged by his impersonal tone and attitude, Betty began voicing more precise threats, drawing still other curt letters from Dan. One, dated on Halloween of 1985, shortly after Dan had finally moved the family out of Coral Reef, warned her about making or carrying out her threats:

> You have told the kids that if I withhold any money this month . . . you will kill me and see that not a brick is left standing in my house . . .
> You better think twice about that. If you make any attack on me or my property, you will never again get a red cent out of me without a court order. You better take a minute to think about the implications of that before you go on a rampage.

Moving to Marston Hills solved several problems at once. Dan finally had the big house he had wanted. The unpleasant memories associated with life in the Coral Reef home could be put in the past. And the new house was not Betty's.

Cypress Avenue is hard to find. One of less than a half-dozen blocks between Richmond Street and the Cabrillo Freeway just before it enters San Diego's world-famous Balboa Park, the tiny enclave of Marston Hills contains large, well-kept homes on spacious lots that are almost invisible from any of the nearby main streets. The homes on the side streets in the surrounding area, known as North Park, are much less expensive. They are lower middle-class, lacking the amenities of trees, lawns, and lush landscaping seen on Cypress and its neighbors.

The location and the neighborhood near downtown San Diego are very different from the subdivisions of suburban La Jolla. Although older and larger than Betty's house overlooking the ocean, Dan's new house cost $85,000 less than hers. When he moved in, he hired a decorator and put up a basketball hoop for his sons over the garage in the back. Linda lived with him openly now.

By the end of 1985 Betty's life had turned inside out. Her children were all living with Dan in the house on Cypress Avenue. Her family home on Coral Reef stood empty. She lived alone in her new house, facing an imminent divorce and an uncertain future.

Bright, interesting, and attractive, she also had some other assets. Betty was college-educated and had a teaching certificate. Sometime during the previous few years, she had also acquired a real estate license. She had loads of friends, contacts throughout La Jolla, and a quick intelligence that could provide opportunities everywhere.

Even people who disliked her described Betty Broderick as energetic and amusing. If her remarks in recent years were often biting and bitter, they were usually funny as well, and she did not lack for male companionship after Dan left her.

She had become friendly that year with Bradley T. Wright, the owner of a fence construction business who was more than five years her junior. Questioned in 1990 about her relationship with Brad by Amy Wallace for the *Los Angeles Times*, Betty denied she was intimate with Wright, although she admitted that he frequently slept at her house and they often took trips together.

Tall and sandy-haired, Wright, an avid sailor, often introduced himself as Betty's boyfriend, but she refused to accept that description. "I never brought Brad anywhere as my date because he was too young," she told Wallace. "I didn't want to be the other half of the mid-life joke."

When Kim and Lee questioned the continuing animosity toward Linda now that she was seeing Brad, Betty responded, "How can you equate the two? Brad doesn't support me!" Kim recalled the answer five years later in the *Los Angeles Times Magazine*.

Wright's presence in her life didn't lessen Betty's anger at Dan Broderick at all. Brian Forbes remembered going for a ride in the used Jaguar she bought herself near the end of the year. The man who considered himself a friend of both Brodericks testified that along the way Betty talked about Dan, saying "she was going to shoot his balls off." Forbes was concerned enough to mention Betty's threat to her target.

With both Dan and Betty gone, the house on Coral Reef was put up for sale in the last months of 1985. In the version Dan gave the *San Diego Reader*, he consulted with Betty on the asking and selling price as well as which real estate agent to use.'

But to Betty, the house was a symbol of her marriage and the proposal to sell it was the most concrete evidence yet that Dan was not coming back. It also meant losing the home she had loved, the first hint of future affluence after the years of debt and hard work. Perhaps most importantly, it was the only financial asset of the Brodericks that included Betty's name on the legal ownership papers.

Daniel Jaffe was then Betty's attorney. He remembered that she was annoyed that Dan had decided to spend $47,000 decorating and landscaping the house to improve the chances of a sale. She considered the money wasted and demanded that half of that expense be added to her half of the selling price of at least $325,000.

One buyer agreed to the minimum, but Betty refused to okay the deal at the last minute, and the prospective home owner didn't want to wait, or go any higher. A second would-be purchaser appeared in January 1986.

Dan Broderick, who now owned a house in Marston Hills and had put up the down payment for Betty's new house in La Jolla, was determined to get the one on Coral Reef off his hands. A meeting was arranged for the end of January.

Daniel Jaffe came down from Los Angeles, although he was already having misgivings about his client. Betty's erratic behavior worried him, and he had not yet received the $10,000 retainer Dan Broderick was supposed to send him. Jaffe still considered himself her lawyer, however, and he was prepared to attend the negotiations and advise Betty. But she refused to be in the same room with Dan and never left the parking lot.

When the attorney brought an agreement down to the car for her to sign, Betty rejected this one also. Daniel Jaffe testified that he warned her then that the house could be sold without her approval if she persisted in blocking a legitimate offer.

"I looked at that house as the only asset," Betty explained to the "Oprah Winfrey" audience years later. "It was indeed the only asset that had my name on it. Nothing else did ever. Dan was fully in control of all the money."

Broderick told the *Reader* he tried to talk Betty into giving her okay over the weekend, even asked her how high the sale price would have to be to get her to agree. He reported that he heard her say "A million dollars wouldn't do it."

Thomas Ashworth, Dan's attorney, went to court the next week for an emergency order, just as Jaffe had predicted. With a judge's permission, the sale went through without Betty's signature or consent on February 4, 1986. Jaffe's office was notified four hours before the closing. She didn't hear about it until afterward.

Betty remembered that she had guests for dinner when she got the telephone call telling her the house on Coral Reef had been sold. She excused herself, saying she would return shortly, but she had to go talk to Dan about something. The dinner guests evidently saw themselves out.

She drove straight to Cypress Avenue, but Dan wasn't home.

"Kim and Lee were there," Betty testified. "I sat out back in a large area near the garage . . . because Dan didn't want me in his house." When he arrived and spotted Betty, she remembered that he paled and immediately ordered her off his property, giving her ten seconds to leave before he called the police.

"I said, 'Wait a minute, I just want some answers,' " Betty recalled. "He didn't want to talk to me . . . I didn't know how much or who he sold it to. How I was going to get my half of the money. I had all kinds of questions. All I had was a phone call, your house had been sold. I needed details."

Dan told her to call her attorney. But Jaffe had returned to Los Angeles, having resigned as her lawyer, still unpaid. (At her trial, the Beverly Hills divorce specialist explained that Dan Broderick was supposed to pay his retainer, but had refused. In matrimonial cases, Jaffe said, it was customary for the spouse who was earning money and wanted the divorce to pay the costs, including attorneys' fees.)

Frightened, frustrated, and furious, Betty drove to the empty house on Coral Reef and tried to stop the sale by setting it on fire. Using a brick, she smashed a glass door, sprinkled gasoline on the stairs, and tossed in a lit match. The fire caused only minor damage, burning spots on the carpeting on the staircase.

By then her emotions had overpowered any rational thinking. The last remnants of that dream of "happily ever after" disappeared with the telephone call that her house had been sold without her approval. That loss added another layer of rage and grief to the enormous burden she was already carrying.

When tragedy strikes, many people search through books and consult gurus, hunt for coincidence and blame fate for explanations of their loss and the cause of their bad luck. Betty thought that she knew exactly where to look for the source of hers.

Nothing in her education or upbringing had prepared Betty Broderick for the feelings of abandonment, betrayal, and anxiety she was experiencing. As an adult, she had known only one haven when she was troubled, and she tried once more to find the security she had been used to. Or at least an explanation of why this was happening to her.

"I had no one to talk to," she said later in court. "I just wanted to talk to Dan."

Betty returned to Marston Hills, determined to make Dan Broderick speak to her. She drove up the circular driveway "extremely hysterical, totally upset, crying," and rammed her van into the front door of the brick house.

"It sounded like a chain saw and everything started shaking," Kim Broderick testified. She had been fixing dinner with her father and a brother in the kitchen when Betty's Suburban barreled into the entrance. Dan ran to the front door and Kim grabbed her brother and hid in the backyard canyon abutting Balboa Park. The teenager was sure her mother "was going to chain-saw Dad."

Five years later Betty tried to explain what she was feeling that evening when she aimed her car at Dan Broderick's front door.

> "The biggest thing that bothered me, besides the sale of the house, was the way he was treating me . . . This is the man who was supposed to take care of us . . . that I trusted and all of that baloney, and I went to him for answers, and the way he treated me was so awful and so cold and so uncommunicative . . . it was just like, screw you, die, get out of my life, go away, he had no respect for me at all."

With the car jammed into the front door pillar, Dan jerked open the driver's side door and grabbed for Betty. She reached under the front seat and pulled out a butcher knife, according to a document in the divorce file. Lee remembered her parents gripping each other by the shoulders, Betty slamming Dan on the head with a heavy key ring. Lee tried to separate the battling adults but "they were squishing me," she testified.

Dan punched Betty in the chest and she fell down. Later she said his blow bruised her sternum. The police arrived. Kim remembered arriving at the scene in time to see her mother sitting handcuffed in the backseat and, as the patrol car drove off, "she stuck her tongue out at me."

Betty was taken to the San Diego County Mental Health Hospital nearby. She was transferred to a private hospital a day later, but kept under observation a full three days. Dan later sent her a bill for the hospitalization. She remembered that she ran into someone at the hospital she had met before, one of the therapists.

Dan had taken her to the therapist's office when they were still together, Betty said. She thought that they were going for counseling on their marital problems. When they arrived, Dan dropped her off, saying she was the one who needed help, not him. She refused to go in alone. She didn't see the therapist again until she ended up in the hospital under observation for trying to drive her car through Dan's front door.

Two years later, talking to reporters for the *San Diego Reader*, Betty expressed no sense of shame or embarrassment about the ramming incident or its aftermath:

> "I'd do it again, only I'd do it better. I was *mad!* He had just stolen everything from me. Up until that point, he had stolen my furniture and my kids and my dogs and my jewelry and my clothes, but I still knew I owned half that house. My name was on that house, and I didn't really understand how it could be taken from me."

The fire damage at the Coral Reef house was only minimal, a broken door and some burned patches on the stairs. At Cypress Avenue, the destruction was more serious and required immediate repairs, forcing a delay in the refurbishing already under way.

Linda Stout, Dan's decorator, ordered new locks for all of the doors, but said he didn't want a new security system. She remembered that Dan had hired a guard to watch the house for a few weeks: "I was stopped several times . . . I also have blond hair and am approximately the same age as [Betty Broderick] so they would stop me and ask me to identify myself."

Dan wanted to make sure Betty stayed away from his house and children. Faced with the furiously angry woman, he seems to have acted in ways that would only enrage her more. Her defense lawyer would later claim it was done on purpose and was part of a larger plan to discredit and ruin Betty Broderick.

Betty thought she knew what was happening. Her friend Patti had gone through a hard-fought divorce with Dave Monahan, a partner in the law firm where Dan used to work. Patti's attorney had been told of a memo that existed within the firm, detailing the steps to gain "maximum leverage" before filing for divorce.

The Monahans, too, had moved into a rental just before the family house was put on the market. Patricia Monahan's attorney husband also tried other tactics that Betty thought she recognized.

"I saw what Dave Monahan did," Betty recalled during her testimony. "I saw Dan doing similar things to me, and I'd say Dan went to the Dave Monahan divorce school: get rid of assets, not pay taxes, not pay down credit cards, and all the similar things Mr. Monahan did during their divorce."

Betty was working by then in an art gallery and looking for someone to replace Daniel Jaffe, the Beverly Hills attorney who wouldn't work without a retainer. Still half hoping she was just having a bad dream and Dan would soon regain his senses and return, her search for legal talent was desultory. Until July.

Dan had sent all four children away for the summer, first to overnight camps, and then on visits to his relatives. Betty had not been consulted, but she did learn that "he told the children that he was sending them out of town because he was going to do something that would enrage me."

In July 1986 she learned what it was. He was right.

When she was served with papers notifying her of another court appearance, Betty called the judge's chambers and explained that she did not yet have an attorney. She expected the hearing would be postponed. She wasn't even in court on the day Dan Broderick divorced her, eighteen months after he first walked out.

Arguing Betty Broderick had abandoned her children, Dan's lawyer, Tom Ashworth, also brought up her record of vandalism and presented edited tapes of the obscene messages she had left on the answering machine. Dan asked for and was awarded sole custody. Betty did not have any visitation rights. The judge reportedly said he was acting in the best interests of the children until Betty Broderick could get professional counseling.

"I had no right to do anything with them again," Betty said on the witness stand in another court. "I was terminated as a mother. I didn't believe anything like this could happen." When she learned about the court proceeding, Betty remembered, "I couldn't even breathe. I was crying so hard . . . I couldn't stand up."

She quit her job so she could concentrate on finding an attorney and regaining custody of the four children. "There were no teenagers, no drivers, nothing, and they needed a mother and he did not provide a mother. I was the mother by phone and through school as much as I could be without being there," Betty remarked with some hyperbole on "Oprah Winfrey" years later.

By then she may have forgotten that in 1985, when Dan walked out, Kim had just turned fifteen and Lee was a year younger. By the time the divorce was final, Kim did have her driver's license and both girls were certainly old enough to stay alone with their younger brothers without sitters or housekeepers.

Dan, who had missed so many evenings with his children when he was married to Betty, was now spending much more of his time at home. Barely aware of their various needs when they first arrived on his doorstep, he was learning to enjoy them. The housekeepers remembered that he often played basketball by the garage with the boys before dinner.

Betty's vengeful gesture of dropping the four children on his doorstep unannounced had backfired.

Dan had legal custody. Betty never quite understood how that happened. She would insist that he "stole" the children, although she acknowledged she had taken them to his house. She knew that she would have to fight in court to get them back. That meant she would have to find someone as familiar with loopholes and legal shortcuts as Dan was.

His legal abilities were obvious. The July proceeding had been an unusual, rarely used ruling granting the divorce and leaving community property, final custody arrangements, and alimony issues to be determined later.

Formally known as a bifurcation order, Betty called it a "bifornication order." In an interview with Susan Lehman for *Mirabella*, Betty explained that in her view, the ruling was "a way to legally fuck your wife and your girlfriend at the same time."

"He got a piece of paper that said he's completely, finally, totally divorced from me," Betty recalled in an interview with Tom Jarriel. "In exchange, what I got on that day was nothing. I got no support, no alimony, no community property, no visitation and no custody. I got that."

Although she complained bitterly about losing her children, and publicly blamed Dan's tricky legal maneuvers for her current situation, Betty was writing privately in her diary that she didn't want custody of the kids. At her trial she explained that until her financial situation was stable, she didn't feel certain she was able to provide for them: "I had no confidence I had any earning power in the world . . .

"Unless I took the children with a financial settlement where I could be assured that I could raise them and feed them and educate them and house them on more than a day-to-day basis, I was too nervous to have them back in my household like I did in February 'eighty-five when Dan left."

But that seemed to be a no-win situation. Betty's frustration at not being able to see her children pushed her into making outrageous remarks and extravagant demonstrations of her hostility. Whenever she did that, Dan would subtract the fines from his payments to her as punishment, and she would be shakier than ever financially.

Her self-destructive behavior was obvious to everyone who knew her, but they, and she, seemed helpless to stop it. Betty refused to see a therapist of any kind, fearing that Dan would exploit her weakness to rationalize his betrayal of their marriage and use every advantage to prove she was too unstable to have custody of her children.

Daniel Jaffe had resigned as Betty's lawyer nearly nine months earlier, but he remained concerned about her situation. In September 1986 he wrote to Thomas Ashworth suggesting that a legal guardian be named to watch out for her interests.

"Because of the bizarre conduct I'd been hearing about for over a year, I thought the legal system or someone should step in and appoint a guardian for her," Jaffe testified five years later. He said he thought Ashworth, as Dan's attorney, was "morally and ethically" obligated to see that Betty had adequate legal representation. But the divorce was final by then.

No alimony settlement had been ordered by the court, but Dan had agreed to send Betty $9,000 a month as a temporary settlement.

Some of the money went for payments on her house, and the rest disappeared in the cost of fixing it up, and on her general, if extravagant, living expenses and shopping sprees—and in the fines Dan imposed for obscene language or unauthorized visits before she even saw the check.

The obscenities continued, however. Robin Tu'ua worked for Dan as a governess and housekeeper beginning in October 1986. She recalled in court how she picked up the telephone once and overheard a conversation between Betty and her youngest son, Rhett.

"She said she wouldn't see Rhett if Rhett didn't get that cunt out of the house," Tu'ua testified with a grimace as she used the apparently unfamiliar word. "He was completely distraught . . . He went upstairs to the bathroom . . . I told him to open the door . . . He came out holding a scissors and clumps of hair."

Tu'ua's voice broke as she repeated what she had heard the young boy say to her that day: "He said he wanted to get out the pain his mom put in his head." After learning about that incident, Dan Broderick told the governess to turn off the ringers on the telephones and let the answering machine pick up all calls.

The young woman recalled that Betty would drive past the house several times a day. "She had a little white car . . . usually around noon . . . I was there alone . . . I saw it four or five times . . . she'd park in front of the house and just stare at it . . ."

Once, the governess remembered, Betty Broderick parked the car and came into the house: "I was in the kitchen, and I felt someone behind me . . . She was standing there, holding the dog. She said no one cares about him. That wasn't true [because] the boys loved the dog and took good care of him. But she said he was abused . . . and she just . . . walked out and took the dog with her."

When Betty tried to call her children at Cypress Avenue and heard Linda Kolkena's voice on the answering machine message on their phone line, she usually voiced her frustration and rage in no uncertain terms. Dan saved several of those tapes as evidence in the harassment charges he brought against Betty, and they were played again in court at her trial:

"What's this 'We can't come to the phone,' cunt?
You're not supposed to come to the phone at the
house. You're supposed to fuck him at the house and
answer the phone at the office."

Betty sometimes laughed about the vulgarities she used. She knew
they infuriated Dan and she did it purposely, claiming it was her only
way to get back at him. "This has evolved to this ridiculous level of
juvenile language because what else can I do?" she asked the reporters for the *San Diego Reader* in 1988.

Occasionally she expanded her vocabulary of four-letter obscenities
and included a four-letter threat.

On the witness stand Tu'ua related another disturbing incident involving Betty and the two younger children. One afternoon Danny
was alone when he got off the bus from school. He said that his
mother had picked up Rhett. While the governess was on the phone
reporting to Dan, she saw Betty's car in front of the house. Following
his instructions, she picked up the restraining order, called the police,
and went outside.

"I asked Rhett to get out of the car," Tu'ua testified. "Mrs. Broderick started yelling at me, 'You can't order my children around, you
have no say.' She was just in a state, an outrageous state. Rhett looked
over at me and whispered, 'My mom has a butcher knife under the
seat.'"

Tu'ua said that Betty "told me she had a gun in her glove box and
she would kill me." The young woman fled into the house with the
children, afraid for her life. Betty drove off as a police car pulled up.

In October, Dan told Betty her fines amounted to $1300 more than
her monthly check, so she would not be receiving a support check.
He and Linda were gone for most of the month on a trip to Europe.
Betty went to the house on Cypress several times while they were
away.

"My children were on his property," Betty explained on the Winfrey show. "They needed money, they needed food, and I was asked
to come over and help them by the babysitter he left them with."

But when Dan returned, he fined her for the visits. On the first of the month he informed her the November support check would also be cut off. Betty was broke and desperate and, as usual, tried to confront Dan and have it out.

"He said I had ten seconds to get off his property or he was calling the police," Betty remembered. "I tried to call his bluff. I said, 'Get off your property and go where? How am I going to manage?' I didn't think he'd really do it . . . He called the police."

Detective Charlene Igo responded to the call. The San Diego police officer testified that she asked Betty Broderick to leave the property several times. When she refused, Betty was again handcuffed and put in the back of a patrol car. Dan and Linda, dressed for a formal evening, left without a backward glance.

It was Dan's big night. After five terms as a vice-president, he was now president of the San Diego Bar Association. That evening was the association's annual black-tie party, the Blackstone Ball. Betty had been to nearly a dozen of the events, but this time Dan put on his cape and top hat to escort Linda. While Dan and Linda danced and greeted friends and colleagues, Betty spent the next few hours in the local lockup, calling for help.

Gail Forbes remembered getting a phone call that night from the women's jail. Betty sounded "exultant." She wanted Gail to call a local society columnist with the gossip that the new president of the Bar Association had had his ex-wife arrested on the night of his triumph.

Betty didn't remember talking to Gail. She did recall phoning another friend and neighbor for help. Melanie Fuller was too frightened of the neighborhood to go alone down to the jail, so she enlisted Brad Wright in the rescue.

Far from exultant, Betty recalled her overriding emotion was sheer terror when she called Melanie Fuller a second time that evening: "I was so afraid, I didn't want to hang up the phone . . . Someone else in the tank was threatening me . . . She was under the influence or something, and started yelling at me, and I was, 'Melanie, don't hang up . . . don't leave me here.' "

Betty was out of jail before the night was over, but it would not be her last taste of life behind bars.

However frightening that initial experience, it wasn't enough to contain her fury against Dan Broderick and Linda Kolkena. Apparently, the feeling was returned. A few days after that memorable evening, Betty received a photograph in the mail. Scrawled across a Post-It on the picture of Dan and Linda at the Blackstone Ball were the words: "Eat your heart out, bitch."

Betty continued to use vulgar names for them as well, even when talking with her young sons. Her daughters were teenagers by now, but Danny was only ten and Rhett was just seven in 1986.

Before Thanksgiving of that year, Betty had a conversation with her youngest son that was also preserved and replayed at her second trial. The tape showed a woman who seems so involved in her own anger that she is uncaring or unaware that she is talking to a child, sure to be confused and upset by her comments.

Telling the boy that she was having guests for the holiday dinner, Betty is heard saying she wishes Rhett, too, could be with her because "you don't belong in the slums with a cunt." Describing Dan as "a sexual maniac," Betty says she's going to have the police "beat the shit out of him. I'll bring the TV cameras with me."

Later in the tape Betty Broderick tells Rhett, "Maybe you're not dead physically, but you're dead emotionally. Your father is a cold-hearted bastard who's fucking the office cunt."

The conversation ends with Betty arguing that "he's killing you all. He's ruining your lives and killing you. What kind of a parent is that? A very bad one." Then she urges her seven-year-old son to "go fight. Go beat up Daddy."

Betty's friends said in court that she used the obscenities out of frustration at not being able to see or even talk to her children and at their apparent ambivalence about living with their father.

Longtime friend Melanie Cohrs testified about another conversation that she overheard between Betty and Rhett, one where the pain was apparently coming from a different direction: "[He] was on the phone, crying, calling out for his mother, asking for help. He said, 'He's going to hurt me,' and all of a sudden, the phone went dead."

Betty frantically tried to call him back, Cohrs remembered clearly, but reached only an answering machine, prompting her to start cursing "out of frustration." The close friend of Betty's also said the two younger children often expressed their unhappiness at having to return to their father's house in Marston Hills.

"Rhett would cling to his mother and cry, saying, 'I don't want to go back there. It's horrible. I hate it,' " Cohrs repeated, adding that Betty would get very upset. She would try to explain to the boys that she didn't 'have a choice. I'll be put in jail' if she didn't send them back.

As much as she missed having her children around, Betty refused any offers to negotiate different custody arrangements without including alimony and division of community property. She even told one of the interviewers at the mental hospital that she was enjoying the freedom of her life since the divorce, and "he and his girlfriend can take care of [the children]."

Betty argued that she didn't want to be dependent on Dan Broderick's apparently uncertain sense of responsibility toward her and the children. She wanted guarantees from a judge about how much money she was getting each month, and no leeway for Dan to reduce it with fines or other punishments. And she wanted assurances about her time with her children.

Without custody or even visitation rights, Dan controlled when and where and for how long she would be with her children. Betty found it unnerving. The holidays that had always been such important family occasions for her were now unpredictable. She was sure if she expressed a desire to have the children for the holidays, Dan would announce he had already made other plans. When she tried to distract herself with her own friends and ignore the absence of the children, Dan would make them available.

Betty began Thanksgiving Day 1986 preparing a dinner at her home on Calle del Cielo for her guests. The children were at Cypress Avenue for the holiday meal. But sometime later in the day, after dinner, an argument developed between Dan and Linda, and the four young Brodericks turned up at Betty's house.

"They arrived on my lawn at nine at night by taxi," Betty remembered. "They said there had been a fight at Dan's house [and] Linda was calling Dan an asshole." After years of watching their parents' pitched battles, the younger Brodericks easily recognized the signs of incipient hostilities and headed for a safe hideout.

Betty may have been hoping this first hint of open dissension in the new Broderick household signified a widening rift, but it was not to be. Whatever the cause of the Thanksgiving night argument, Dan and Linda managed to work it out.

November 1986 had been a difficult month for all of the Brodericks. Betty, more serious and scared since her arrest the evening of the Blackstone Ball, hired J. William Hargreaves, a local lawyer who often worked as a divorce mediator. She had wanted to try mediation earlier, but backed off when Dan refused to pay for it. Now she went to Hargreaves to fight for her share of the community property and a fair alimony settlement.

"I felt I was forced to get into court and fight with Dan Broderick," Betty said. "I had no choice . . . it was the second holiday season I didn't have the children."

She could have spent that Christmas with her sons and daughters, but her determination not to give an inch to Dan and Linda ended that opportunity. He had suggested that she take the children skiing that vacation, and even offered her $2000 toward expenses. But Betty wanted to rent a condominium that cost three grand for the week, and Dan refused to give her any more money to take them away. She had no money of her own left to pay for the trip, so Betty spent the holidays without them.

The year ended as the one before had. Now officially divorced, Betty was alone in her house near the ocean. Dan and Linda and the four children were living on Cypress Avenue. There still had been no final settlement on custody, alimony, or community property. But now Betty claimed to be prepared to go to court to fight for her rights.

7

Broderick v. Broderick

Finding the "killer attorney" she felt she needed wasn't easy. Betty Broderick wasn't happy with Bill Hargreaves. He wanted her to go for custody of the children, but despite her complaints that Dan "stole" her kids, she wasn't really interested in making that fight seriously.

"She felt that, since Dan had taken certain steps in leaving her, he should have the responsibility of keeping the children," Hargreaves testified.

She again tried a lawyer in Los Angeles. According to the *San Diego Reader*, Betty still didn't have the cash for a retainer. When she met the new attorney, he accepted the gold and diamond necklace she was wearing instead.

Before the lawyer cum jeweler could get very far, he, too, was fired. Betty had met Tricia Smith, a woman attorney who kept her office in Del Mar and wasn't well known in San Diego.

Betty was impressed and told the *Reader*: "She's great . . . she's tall and thin and classy and smart. And the reason nobody knows her downtown is she settles everything."

Smith's first order of business was trying to get a court-ordered temporary alimony judgment. In the nearly two years since Dan had left her, Betty had developed compulsive habits of both eating and shopping. Food was relatively easy to get, but money was chronically short in Betty's house and bank accounts.

Early in 1987 Betty was officially awarded temporary support payments of $16,000 a month. Dan immediately appealed the ruling as too high.

Betty also appealed, but she argued that she should be getting much more. Dan earned $1.2 million in 1986. His monthly spendable income was $48,000. She had supported him during the lean years when he was acquiring his skills, and she had been his social partner in the more recent years of politics and parties that now garnered such enormous fees. She thought at least half his earnings, or $25,000 a month, was not unreasonable considering her contribution.

After the long years of struggle and hardship, he was going to spend his money on someone else, and Betty wanted to be sure she got her share. Most of her divorced friends had received ridiculously low settlements, in Betty's opinion. Patti Monahan, for example, got only $32,000 a year from her ex-husband, a senior partner in San Diego's top law firm. That was not going to happen to Elisabeth Broderick.

Although the court-ordered payments totaled $192,000 a year, Betty insisted it wasn't enough to maintain the lifestyle she was accustomed to. That had included $2000 designer dresses and $8000 ball gowns. Five thousand of the monthly $16,000 went for the mortgage and taxes on her house with the ocean view. Then there were the expenses of pool maintenance, a maid, and a gardener. Much of the rest apparently was spent refurbishing her wardrobe as her weight and clothes size fluctuated.

Perhaps because she was used to cooking for a family of six, perhaps because she was bored and lonely, perhaps because she was depressed, perhaps because she was angry—whatever the reason, Betty had a weight problem for the first time in her life. Her youngest daughter noticed the difference and became concerned about her mother's health.

"She got fat," Lee testified. "She had never been fat. Before they were separated, she was thin. She used bad language. I was afraid she would hurt herself."

Melanie Cohrs commented that after 1985 she "didn't seem to care as much about her appearance." Marilyn Olson also saw a change from a "good-looking, charming, articulate lady" to one who "was very fearful for her future" and showed a "basic loss of control."

Someone was apparently trying to take advantage of Betty's growing insecurities. The mail at Calle del Cielo brought anonymous envelopes with advertisements for diet products and wrinkle cream. Betty was sure that Linda Kolkena was to blame for them. An investigation by the defense team turned up a Kolkena friend who allegedly remembered mailing some envelopes for Linda but never saw what was inside them.

Everyone noticed the weight Betty had gained—nearly sixty pounds—and most of her friends were also aware of her shopping sprees. In 1986 she spent more than $37,000 on clothes and accessories; she explained that she had to replace the things ruined by the rats in the rental house.

Longtime friend Patti Monahan remembered that Betty bought a $40,000 lynx fur coat after Dan moved out, even though San Diego nights rarely get below fifty degrees. Helen Pickard recalled that Betty received catalogues so she could start buying clothes early in the morning before the West Coast stores were open. She remembered seeing high-priced clothes hanging in Betty's closet, "with tags that hadn't even been cut off."

The new clothes didn't ease the anger that still burned inside of her. In March 1987 the Brodericks made appointments with Ruth Roth, a psychologist who tried to mediate the custody dispute between them. Roth testified at Betty's trials about her impressions of those sessions. She said she found Betty Broderick uncooperative.

"I'm not going to be a single parent of four kids," Roth quoted from notes she had made on March 3, 1987, their first meeting. "He'll die first."

About the children, she had noted that Betty said, "The less I see them or hear from them, the better . . . No bother, no kids."

A week later Roth met again with Betty and again took notes on their session. After repeating her comments of the previous meeting, Betty added, "I'm not letting go that easy. The little fuckhead was mine and he'll stay mine."

When Roth expressed concern about the threats she was hearing, Betty responded, "I threaten the fuckhead all the time." Roth testified that she notified Dan Broderick of Betty's comments, breaking the confidentiality of the sessions with Betty because she felt there was a real danger to him.

In their final discussion, the psychologist said, Betty again refused to discuss custody issues with her, saying instead, "I don't want to have kids as a single mother. I won't let you talk me into it." Roth described Betty Broderick as "the angriest person I ever saw."

Everyone who knew Betty was aware of her rage. She talked to friends constantly about her problems and her feelings of being persecuted. But it was the children who bore the brunt of the fury she felt toward their father.

That same month, March 1987, Betty had a long, wrenching conversation with her son Danny, then about eleven years old. Kim Broderick testified that her father began taping the call when he overheard his son sobbing while talking to his mother.

This is a partial transcription of that conversation. The entire tape lasted thirty-four minutes when it was played in court:

DANNY: This whole thing could be settled. If you don't stop saying bad words, it will never be settled, Mom.

BETTY: You tell Daddy to settle it quick before lunchtime tomorrow . . .

DANNY: No, you have to settle it before lunchtime tomorrow.

BETTY: Why?

DANNY: [*crying*] You're the only one that can change . . . No one else can change it except you . . .

BETTY: No, I mean the settlement. He's got all the money, he's got every single cent the two of us own. When he gives me half, then we'll discuss—

DANNY: [*crying*] He gives you money every—I don't know . . . but he gives you a *lot* of money.

BETTY: [*grudgingly*] Yeah, well, it's not enough.

DANNY: Why isn't it enough?

BETTY: It's not what the law says I own.

DANNY: How much do you own?

BETTY: Half.

DANNY: You'd get your stupid money if you'd just stop saying bad words.

For the next few exchanges, Betty tries to change the subject and ask him about school and what he's been doing, but Danny keeps reverting back to her bad words—and someone can be heard talking to him in the background and briefly on the phone.

DANNY: How come you won't stop saying bad words?

BETTY: Because I'm mad.

DANNY: Yeah, well how can you be mad for two years? And you're just going to get worse and worse and worse until you get your stupid share of money, and you're never going to get your stupid share of money unless you stop saying bad words!!!! (*said in a rising voice, slightly hysterically*) . . . There's nothing funny about it, Mom.

BETTY: Where's Daddy while you're yelling at me like this? He's probably listening.

DANNY: I don't know . . . walking through the room every once in a while to fix some light bulbs.

BETTY: Where's the cunt?

DANNY: Nowhere, Mom. I don't know.

BETTY: It's not time to come over and screw him yet, huh?

DANNY: She's with her family . . .

BETTY: [*in a high-pitched voice*] Oh, with her family . . . I wonder what her family thinks of her fucking her boss who's married with four kids.

DANNY: Not anymore, Mom.

BETTY: Well, what did they think of her when she was fucking him when he was married with four kids?

DANNY: I don't know . . . Why do you keep using bad words until you get your stupid money share? Well, you're not going to get it, Mom . . .

BETTY: You comfortable in that house?

DANNY: Why do you keep on doing it?

BETTY: Because I'm ticked off.

DANNY: Okay, you've told me a million times . . . you're ticked off, who cares? You'd better stop saying bad words or else you're going to be more ticked off.

BETTY: [*giggles*] No matter what bad words I say, I still own half.

DANNY: Fine, after you stop saying bad words, you're going to get your stupid half.

BETTY: You're a little monster . . .

DANNY: You're not listening to me . . .

BETTY: I'm listening. You're giving me an earache, yelling in my ear.

DANNY: [*crying*] Why do you do it? . . . Because you're being self-ish, you want everything, you want to get all the kids, you want to get all the money, you want to get him away from Linda, and you want to still say bad words . . . It's not going to work, Mom.

BETTY: Just remember, you have no business to be mad at me. I didn't cause any of this. Daddy did. He caused . . .

DANNY: You're causing it to be worse and worse . . .

BETTY: . . . He caused all this trouble and you're mad at me and I did nothing, absolutely nothing.

DANNY: I'm mad at you because you're doing something right now, you're not letting us come over to see you. You're just wanting all your money.

BETTY: What do you mean I'm not letting you come over here?

DANNY: [*hysterically*] It's you . . . You're saying the bad words.

BETTY: I'd rather say a bad word than be a bad word . . . Dan and Linda are bad words!!

DANNY: Fine. You can say what you want, but you're just being a real jerk about this family and no one will like you anymore.

BETTY: Thanks a lot.

DANNY: [*sobbing*] Well . . . we don't even know what you sound like or look like if you keep saying those stupid bad words.

BETTY: Well, I didn't do any of this . . .

DANNY: [*crying*] You're doing something right now. You're saying those stupid bad words and you're not making any sense . . .

BETTY: Daddy fucked me over . . . my whole life . . .

DANNY: You're doing the same thing right now, Mom, you're making it a whole lot worse, too.

BETTY: No, I'm not.

DANNY: You're saying bad words, and nothing is ever going to happen if you keep on saying bad words.

BETTY: Saying bad words has nothing to do with fucking the family.

DANNY: I know, but it has to do with messing up the whole family, because if you don't stop saying bad words, he's not going to let us come over there—ever, so you'd better stop doing it or you're just going to make your whole family mad at you—everybody who wants to come over there.

BETTY: [*cries*]

DANNY: Why don't you stop? Huh? *(crying and sobbing can be heard)* You're always saying that you're not doing anything, but you are, Mom. Get off the phone!

FEMALE VOICE: Who are you talking to?

DANNY: Mom. Get off the phone!

FEMALE VOICE: Don't yell at me.

DANNY: No, I am going to yell at you! Get off the phone!! You would make it a lot easier for everyone in this family if you'd just stop saying bad words! You're going to get your stupid share if you stop saying bad words. You're going to get the kids that want to go to your house, forever, if you just stop saying stupid bad words!! Mom, will you just stop? Mom?

BETTY: I hate Daddy.

DANNY: It's not going to do any good to keep saying bad words.

BETTY: [*crying*] We had such a nice family.

DANNY: I know, but you're just going to make it worse by saying bad words, Mom.

BETTY: We had the best family [*her voice rises sharply*] in the whole world and we were all so happy. All the kids and me were all so happy.

DANNY: I know, and we'll all be a lot happier if you just stop saying bad words . . .

BETTY: You tell that slimeball—

DANNY: See what I mean, Mom? You're saying it right now, and you'd better stop or else you're just going to make everything worse.

BETTY: You tell that slimeball to act like a man.

DANNY: He is acting like a man. Okay, what's he doing wrong, Mom? You're the person that's—who's doing the thing wrong—and you're saying bad words and making the family even worse.

BETTY: I'm not saying bad words for no reason.

DANNY: I know, but still you have no right to say a bad word in front of your kids. You gave us to him . . . twice. It was really stupid . . . and you got mad, and it wasn't even his fault that we got over there, and now you say bad words and we're going to stay over here for the rest of our lives if you don't stop it. [crying]

BETTY: Maybe you should stay there the rest of your life . . .

DANNY: We don't want to, though, Mom. We want to live with you, but you're just making it harder for all of us that want to live over there. If you stop saying bad words, everyone will be happier. At least, I know I will. And I know Rhett will. You probably don't care because all you want is your money. Why won't you just stop saying the bad words?

BETTY: Poor little boy. I'm crying, too.

DANNY: Why won't you just stop saying them? You've said them millions of times, you don't need to say them anymore.

BETTY: Danny, he's absolute scum. He's cheated and lied and fucked around. There's nothing—

DANNY: You've been mad for two years now. That's long enough, Mom. You should have been done after two months of it instead of two years.

BETTY: I would have been done in two hours if we had a settlement and Daddy did this like a gentleman . . .

DANNY: [indistinguishable]

BETTY: . . . throwing me in jail and stealing my house out from under me . . .

DANNY: He threw you in jail because you came and ran through his house . . .

BETTY: After he stole my house from me.

DANNY: He didn't steal your house. That was a rented house.

BETTY: No, Coral Reef. The day he sold Coral Reef and kept the money.

DANNY: Because you threw gasoline all over it.

BETTY: You don't understand these things, Danny.

DANNY: You don't either, Mom. You better stop saying the bad words.

BETTY: Tell your father to grow up and act like a gentleman and this could all be over in an hour.

DANNY: Well, you should grow up and act like a woman and stop being so mad about all this, and you just have to stop saying the bad words and you won't. You're being a jerk, you're being selfish. You want everything your way. And you're not going to get everything your way if you don't stop saying bad words.

BETTY: I haven't had anything my way.

DANNY: I know, but you're not going to get it. You want it, though, but you're not going to get it until you stop saying bad words. You'll get it, not all of it, but you're going to get some of it at least, but you have to stop.

In other conversations, Betty was reported to have encouraged the boys to use her vulgar terms when talking to Linda and Dan.

Neither adult Broderick seemed able to abstain from putting the children into the middle of their personal fight. Dan Broderick refused to speak to his wife and told his children that he didn't want to hear her voice.

Even when he went to Betty's house to pick them up, he did all he could to avoid meeting her. He would call ahead on his car phone to alert them. On arrival, Dan would honk his horn. The kids would come out so he didn't see or speak to Betty. At his own home he called her names in front of the children and to some extent held them responsible for her conduct.

Lee testified that her father often told her brothers to ask their mother "if she was crazy . . . why didn't she go to the doctor?" The younger boys were told "if she did go to see a doctor, they'd be able to see her more often." Betty accused Dan of holding the children "hostage" to her actions.

Betty's erratic and increasingly violent behavior certainly indicated a very troubled and angry woman, but it is unlikely that taunting her with words like "crazy" was the best way to encourage her to seek help. Neither, it appeared, was dragging her into court.

Defense attorney Jack Earley, who had access to Betty's records and the divorce file, counted thirty-seven different notices, legal filings, and other papers, sent to her in the first six months of 1987, averaging more than one a week.

She had continued her unannounced visits to Dan's house on Cypress. In May she was sentenced to nearly a month in prison on contempt of court charges for violating the restraining order keeping her away from Dan and his property. The actual time she spent at the Las Colinas jail for women in Santee was eventually reduced to not much more than a week. The tiny concrete cells were a big comedown from the five-bedroom houses in La Jolla.

"What else can you do?" Daniel Broderick asked in a taped interview played on ABC's "20/20" after his death. "I mean, repeated warnings—'Stop this, you can't do this, leave the guy alone'—and she would come back and do it again. And pretty soon the judge had to say, 'Well ma'am, what do you expect here? This is a law-abiding society. You cannot act like this. Stop it.' And he put her in jail."

By then Betty had also made the rounds of various organizations, associations, and offices established to help abused women. She didn't really fit into any of the categories those groups were designed to aid. Her strongest support came from the members of HALT— Help Abolish Legal Tyranny—a citizens' group critical of the legal system. That's where she met Ronnie Brown and Dian Black, and they often accompanied Betty to court during the long divorce proceedings.

Betty often spoke about her legal troubles to other HALT members, and she soon became active in its discussions and organization. She complained that Dan's standing in the legal community won him preferential treatment in court. Judges greeted him by name, she said, and allowed him to use a special entrance to elude reporters.

She explained how he would "come in through the judge's entrance and be in the judge's office every morning talking to the judge."

She accused Dan of avoiding other responsibilities as well. In the spring of 1987 Kim had a big date for the high school prom, but her father refused to pay more than a hundred dollars for a prom dress, according to a story Betty told the *San Diego Reader*. Kim went to her mother "just sobbing hysterically."

Betty grabbed her daughter, keys, and charge card and set off to the rescue at "ten to nine the night before the prom." She headed for the exclusive and expensive Lillie Rubin shop in La Jolla Village, arriving as they were locking up.

"I knock on the door 'cause they know me, and I'm like, 'My God, she needs a dress for tomorrow,' " Betty said. The one they chose— "V-neck, long-sleeved, beaded peach taffeta"—was a size too large. By calling around the country, the clerk located a size six in Florida and for an extra $47 Betty had it delivered by Federal Express.

"It was here by three o'clock the next day," she recalled. "I kept her home from school. I got her nails done. I gave her my pearls. I had her out the door at all costs. That's how I am about my kids."

But she wanted to be that way in the family setting she had always known. Over and over Betty told her friends and her lawyers that she would not be a single mother. Dan would be free of all parental duties but the financial one if she had custody. Without the children around, he and Linda would be free to enjoy all the pleasures that Betty felt she had earned.

Always short of money for herself, Betty also resented having to pay for clothing and shoes for the children when she didn't have responsibility for them. The issue came up again that fall after she decided that Rhett and Danny needed new clothes for upcoming holiday parties and dance classes.

Betty recounted choosing "nothing fancy . . . navy-blue blazer, gray pants, brown loafers, button-down shirts, ties, a belt . . . and two ski jackets. One each," for a total of $800. She said she offered to split the bill with Dan "even though I have no child support, and that was nice of me . . ."

Dan refused to pay for the clothes, and Betty wouldn't pay the full bill. Eight months after her shopping trip, the *San Diego Reader* reported the store was still waiting to be paid.

November 7, 1987, was Betty's fortieth birthday, and her friends decided a party would get her mind off her problems. Nearly two dozen women gathered for the surprise party at the pricey George's at the Cove Restaurant in La Jolla.

Some of the guests were members of the investment club Betty had started to help her understand her financial position; they met each month at the house on Calle del Cielo. One of them, Judy Backhaus, told reporters shortly after Betty was arrested, that she had seemed "very touched" by the party and the affection shown by her friends who were at the restaurant that day.

"Although many felt worn-out and burdened by the task of trying to get Betty on with her life," Backhaus said, "it was evidenced by the women there that they did want to help her bring in her forties, hoping that possibly things could turn around and she could get on with her life."

Betty was finding that difficult. Her rage at Dan and the unpredictable turn her life had taken seemed to color everything she thought and did. She had been keeping a diary for nearly three years, and at the end of 1987 the entries were as bitter as ever.

Dan had offered to give her custody of the children, but Betty saw that as a "tactic" to gain himself freedom. She also didn't think her house, undergoing extensive repairs and rehabilitation, was "fit" for children. Further, her own spending habits had been getting more and more extravagant and she didn't think she was getting enough money to pay for herself, let alone the needs of four children.

Perhaps to ease the passage into undeniable middle age on her fortieth birthday, Betty wrote checks totaling nearly $10,000 in November and early December. She paid department stores, credit card companies, and jewelers. Whatever she shopped for and bought in those months wasn't enough to keep her occupied, however.

The new year brought a new court hearing for Betty. Dan again accused her of violating the restraining order by coming to the house on Cypress. Betty explained to the *San Diego Reader* that she was just dropping off the dog before she left on a vacation to Tahiti, but she was fined $8000. The judge warned her that the next time she was found in contempt, she'd have to pay Dan's legal fees as well.

It was not long after that latest dispute that Betty wrote in her diary of her bottomless rage at Dan and the helpless frustration of not being in control of her life:

> There is no better reason in the world for some-
> one to kill than to protect their home, possessions,
> and family from attack and destruction. You have
> attacked and destroyed me, my home, my posses-
> sions, and my family . . . You're the sickest person
> alive. A law degree does not give you license to kill
> and destroy, nor does it give you immunity from
> punishment. No one will ever mourn you.

Betty blamed Dan for everything that had gone wrong. His demand to end their marriage had destroyed the family she had nurtured. The children were showing signs of the continued stress and disruption in their lives. Being pawns in the unending struggle between Dan and Betty to checkmate each other was beginning to take its toll on all four of them.

Lee was back living with her mother most of the time. Under the emotional demands of the divorce and custody battles, the teenager had briefly developed a drug problem that led to her dropping out of high school. Dan became angry and disowned his daughter, formally writing her out of his will when he amended it that August. Lee moved to Calle del Cielo with Betty. Dan had also wanted Kim to move out after her eighteenth birthday, but later he agreed to pay her college tuition.

The younger boys were in and out of therapy. Dan claimed that their psychologists did not want them to see Betty, but "they want to be with their mom." They spent many weekends at Calle del Cielo, even if no official visitation rights had been established.

Betty had bought a cellular phone so the children, especially her sons, could always reach her. She called them several times a day as well. Sometimes she got through to them, sometimes she got the machine. She resented any barrier, even one she helped construct. Throughout the spring, Betty often expressed her fury and defiance in the messages she left on the answering machine at Cypress Avenue.

Not all the messages were obscene, Lee testified. But if Betty couldn't get through to her sons or heard Linda's voice on the machine, she would use every vulgar word she could think of. Dan made copies of the coarser messages and brought them with him in May 1988 for still another contempt of court hearing against Betty.

In one she calls Dan a "fucking insane asshole" and accuses him of spending another "drunken afternoon with the office cunt." On another, Betty can be heard saying, "I'm having so much fun! I love this machine! I want to go to court to prove that you're a fuckhead and she's a cunt. This is so much fun!"

Betty was fined again. Family Court Judge Anthony Joseph wanted to sentence her to jail. Dan Broderick earned himself a judicial dressing-down by suggesting leniency, the judge warning Broderick not to bring another harassment charge unless he was ready to agree to a prison sentence. (One judge, probably Joseph, also warned Dan that "the girlfriend's voice is not to be used on the answering machine, which is a tool for the mother and children to communicate.")

For her part, Betty regarded the time that she spent in court as "a colossal waste of taxpayer money to accomplish nothing," and, unwilling to admit any responsibility for her actions, considered herself to be further harassed by Dan's legal maneuvering. To some extent the constant contempt proceedings appear to be an effort to control Betty —a legal way of saying, "Be a good little girl and don't complain and Daddy will be nice to you, but if you don't do exactly as you're told, you'll be punished."

By now the Broderick divorce was taking on legendary status. Betty had been all over southern California talking to groups campaigning for divorce reform, changes in the legal system, and related areas. She had badgered reporters regularly with her accounts of the preferential treatment accorded Dan Broderick in court, her inability to find an attorney and the consequences to her and her children.

Two reporters for the weekly *San Diego Reader* were interested enough to probe further. Paul Kreuger and Jeannette De Wyze spent several hours talking to Betty and Dan in the summer of 1988. They also chased down the lawyers who had briefly represented Betty, and they talked to people around the court.

A long article was prepared for publication in July, but never appeared. Although he had agreed to the interviews, Dan Broderick changed his mind and threatened to sue the weekly for invasion of privacy if the story was published. The paper backed off on the advice of its lawyers, and the original story was killed. (A short one about Dan's success in keeping the divorce files confidential appeared after the divorce trial, and a second, longer article, based on the original interviews, was published after Betty's arrest.)

Perhaps Dan was worried about the effect an article about his long-delayed divorce settlement would have on his public image. Even discounting much of Betty's complaints, as the writers do, he does not look very heroic in the saga of their marriage and separation. Her very vocal complaints about his attitude and action attracted negative attention, not the respect he wanted. And the accusation of mid-life crisis may have struck a raw nerve.

At any rate, Dan chose to neutralize one of Betty's most telling arguments in a very public and flamboyant way. In September, five years after he had first hired her as an assistant in his legal office, he proposed to Linda Kolkena. According to the San Diego newspapers, he chose a downtown restaurant, Dobson's, as the setting, and the traditional method, down on one knee, as the medium.

The audio tape of that 1988 interview was played on "20/20" during a report on Betty's trial. Dan Broderick described his attraction to the woman who was about to become his fiancée: "As pretty as Linda is, her looks are not her best quality. She has the most wonderful, pleasant, sweet disposition of any woman I've ever known. I really mean that."

Betty had long complained about their public flaunting of the teaching of the Catholic Church and the example they were setting for the Broderick children. Now they planned to marry. Dan and Linda would no longer be living in sin, and Betty could no longer hold even a fantasy that Dan would return someday.

On one of her illegal but apparently unpreventable prowls through the house on Cypress Avenue, she found a half-finished letter Linda was writing to Dan's parents, expressing happiness over her engagement. Betty took the letter and replaced it with her own message to her former in-laws: a four-page complaint about the way Dan had treated her.

Criminal attorney Jack Earley said the divorce file resembled a negligence suit, not a marital dispute. There were more court appearances, meetings for the mandatory settlement conference, and hearings on the arguments over community property and alimony payments.

That fall there was still another court hearing, this one on Dan's demand that Betty undergo vocational testing. She considered this just another delay tactic, and said later she agreed to the requirement to speed up the process. Tricia Smith no longer represented her, so Betty acted as her own attorney, saying she wanted to select her own counselor. She named a respected professional in La Jolla, and the judge agreed.

At their first meeting, Betty told the vocational counselor to arrange payment with Dan's attorney, now Gerald Barry, Jr., since Tom Ashworth's appointment as presiding judge of Family Court had come through. The plan for vocational testing fell apart, according to Betty, because Dan wanted access to the results if he was going to pay. The La Jolla counselor was uncomfortable with the breach of confidentiality and refused to the terms, so no agreement on payment could be reached.

In November, Betty again decided to approach Dan directly and try to get something settled. Carrying her cellular phone to call Dian Black if she was arrested again, Betty drove to Marston Hills and found Dan outside gardening.

He was surprised to see her, but listened as she told him she wanted to settle their dispute. Linda, seeing Betty from a window, offered to call the police, but he waved her off. Instead, Dan avoided

Betty's immediate demands. He said he didn't have the necessary figures with him and promised he would call her the next day. Betty drove away.

Dan never called. Fed up and determined to get a final judgment, Betty approached Judge Joseph and asked him to set a trial date. It was scheduled for the last week in December. Sometime before the Brodericks got to court, the file of motion papers, responses, and subpoena service notices disappeared from the clerk's office.

Betty, accompanied by Dian Black, was acting as her own lawyer. She brought in papal blessings and other mementoes of her marriage as "tangible proof of what Dan had promised." She claimed later that she didn't get a fair hearing because the missing papers were all her handwritten responses to Dan's charges over the years. The presiding judge denied the missing papers were important to his decision.

At Gerald Barry's request, the proceedings were closed to the press and public. After most of the missing papers had been re-created, the entire divorce file was permanently sealed at the request of both parties. The judge said any publicity might cause psychological harm to the Broderick children. As a result, only Betty's side of the story can be known. Dan's version remains unviewed in the files at his own insistence.

In fact, the *San Diego Reader*, which had been watching for it, reported the hearing in late 1988 never appeared on the daily court calendar, either. The weekly newspaper's reporters also missed Dan Broderick's appearance because he was allowed to use the rear exit normally reserved for judges and security problems.

Four years after Dan first walked out, a final judgment was going to be made on community property, custody of the children, and alimony. Betty questioned Dan herself during the hearing and remembered him saying that he thought she wanted his "death and ruination."

"I laughed," she said at her trial for his murder. "He was obviously a fool."

Dan had made a similar comment the year before while talking to reporters from the *San Diego Reader*. In their January 1989 article about the secret proceedings in the Broderick divorce, Paul Krueger and Jeannette De Wyze quote him as saying the current trial may settle some long-standing issues, but, "It's not going to end this thing.

"It's not going to end until one of us is gone," Dan reportedly said in the summer of 1988, more than a year before he was killed.

Papers filed during that January hearing show Dan Broderick was grossing more than $110,000 a month from his law practice. He claimed to net over $67,000 against living expenses of less than $33,000. Betty put her monthly living costs at just over $27,000. She also mentioned legal bills totaling more than $500,000.

Family Court judge William Howatt questioned the four Broderick children in private. Kim later testified that she told the judge that Betty "was obsessed with hatred" for Dan. Lee and Kim were over eighteen and no longer considered children, but Judge Howatt's ruling in March awarded custody of the boys, still minors, to their father.

The previous summer, Dan had told the *San Diego Reader* interviewers: "I do not think it would be in their best interest to live with her, and honestly I don't think it's in their best interest to spend any time with her either . . . But I can't separate them from her altogether."

When Betty pulled one of her outrageous stunts, Dan would restrict her access to her sons. Danny and Rhett wanted to see their mother, though, and, after a couple of weeks Betty would promise Dan that her behavior would be acceptable and that she would not bring them back unexpectedly. He said he found it difficult to resist their entreaties and would let them see her again. Or at least until she did something else he didn't like.

For the rest, Betty got half the proceeds from the sale of the house on Coral Reef, pension funds from Dan's law firm, and a court-ordered alimony of $16,100 a month. A detailed list of personal property was carefully divided up between the two of them. The judge also renewed the restraining order keeping her one hundred yards away from the house on Cypress Avenue.

As usual, it had no effect on Betty. On one of her surreptitious visits, she apparently came across a list of the people being invited to the outdoor ceremony planned for the next month. Already furious that Dan was marrying Linda twenty years to the month after her own wedding, Betty carried off the guest list.

After hearing from some of the invited guests about threatening phone calls they had received from Betty, Dan and Linda went back to court demanding that she return the list and stop her menacing calls. The notice of the hearing was only four hours, and Betty claimed she had to leave her job without warning to obey the order.

When Linda discovered that Betty was contacting some of the people invited to her wedding, she retaliated. Driving to Calle del Cielo, she convinced Maria Montes to let her in while Betty was away. While looking for her wedding list, Linda allegedly took Betty's diary.

"I felt emotionally attacked and assaulted," Betty told Kathleen Neumeyer in the *Ladies Home Journal.* "I had no way to defend myself." So on March 14 she bought a five-shot, .38-caliber revolver. It wasn't completely unfamiliar. Betty had fired a gun a few times on school-sanctioned trips when she was a child, but she had never owned a handgun before.

Long before she bought it, there had been stories about Betty having a gun. Two years earlier, Robin Tu'ua had been threatened with one, but hadn't seen it. Neither had Brian Forbes when he recalled Betty's threat to shoot Dan's private parts.

Everyone who knew her had heard her say at one time or another that she was going to kill Dan Broderick. When she did buy a handgun, Betty made no secret of her purchase, getting a legal permit and telling her friends about it.

Concerned about Betty's intentions at the wedding, Linda and Dan's brother wanted him to wear a bullet-proof vest at the ceremony planned for the front lawn on Cypress Avenue, but Dan rejected their advice. A man who refused to wear a rented tuxedo at his first wedding was not about to spoil the cut of a custom-made jacket at his second.

After hearing of Betty's threats from so many directions, he did hire guards and warned them his ex-wife might show up with a gun. He didn't really believe that, however, and told some friends that Betty wouldn't kill "the golden goose" who was paying her bills.

Betty's friends had worked out their own scheme to protect everybody. Helen Pickard spent more than sixteen hours with Betty on April 22, the day of the wedding. If Betty managed to leave her sight, she was prepared to beep one of the guests at the reception by the backyard pool on Cypress Avenue. Nothing happened that day.

But the marriage seemed to make Betty angrier than ever. Dan and Linda's honeymoon, sailing on a small boat through the Caribbean, was supposed to have been Betty's twentieth anniversary cruise. There were other annoying jabs, too; pinpricks by most standards, but to Betty Broderick they felt like surgery without anesthesia.

No longer the girlfriend, but the wife, Linda again recorded the message on the answering machines. It seemed a low-key way of enforcing her position and reminding Betty that the situation had changed. It also enraged her rival and brought on more obscene responses.

Now that Dan and Linda were married, they had their own china, and Betty wanted her wedding dishes back. They had not been included in the division of community property adjudicated earlier in the year. Linda Kolkena Broderick was inclined to return the china, but she asked a close friend who was a divorce lawyer for advice.

Sharon Blanchet recommended that Linda not respond to Betty's demand. It was the attorney's opinion, based on previous experiences, that no one thing would satisfy Betty Broderick. She would always want something else, find some new demand to make. Linda followed Blanchet's advice and refused to return the china, adding to Betty's resentment.

When Linda ordered her new stationery, that, too, turned into a source of bitterness for Betty, who told Susan Lehman about it for an article in *Mirabella* magazine:

> "She bought exactly the same stationery I had. Of all the stationery in the whole world, why did she have to go to Neiman Marcus and get the same navy-blue and cream-colored stationery with the name Mrs. Daniel T. Broderick the Third written, in the same print, across the top? Mrs. Daniel T. Broderick the Third, that's who I was."

Not anymore. And Betty couldn't seem to accept that.

"It was as though Linda stepped into my life," Betty said in court. "It all kept going—my traditions, my friends, my children—the only difference, the 'what is wrong with this picture' part, is that Linda was there instead of me."

Betty insisted that she bought the gun to protect herself against further intrusions. Its presence fascinated Danny and Rhett. She tried to defuse their interest by taking them to a pistol range and letting them fire the guns there under supervision.

Betty had also tried to cool their ardor for the handgun by showing the .38 to them. Then she had locked it away and gave them her usual admonition, "If you touch this, I'll kill you!" but they searched anyway. Eventually they found it hidden in her bedroom, and Betty moved the weapon to what she considered a safer place—the zippered pouch in the big purse she kept locked in her car.

The boys talked about the gun constantly. Dan heard their chatter. Knowing that Lee spent more time with Betty than the other children, he asked his youngest daughter to find out for sure if there really was a gun. The next time Lee visited at Calle del Cielo, she approached Betty directly, repeating what Danny and Rhett were saying.

"Everybody knows you have a gun, and I want to see it," Lee remembered saying to her mother.

Betty took her to the bedroom door and made her wait outside, Lee recalled. She showed the revolver to her daughter, even offered to take her to a shooting range to learn to use it, then locked it away again, Lee said. The young woman also remembered that once that summer her mother had the gun in a bathrobe pocket when Dan Broderick came to pick up his sons.

"I was deathly afraid of Dan Broderick," Betty explained on the witness stand when asked about the incident. "I was afraid of him attacking me and maligning me and threatening me to take the children and to lose the house and I'd never see another red cent from him."

During the summer of 1989 Betty found another lawyer and decided to go back to court to try for custody of Danny and Rhett. Dan and Linda were away a lot, leaving the boys with a housekeeper. Betty had to get a judge's okay to have them stay with her instead. The custody hearing was postponed with Dan's absences, although he had promised to have the issue resolved in time for the start of school in September.

By October there was still no date for a hearing, and Dan and Linda were off again late in the month. This trip seemed to be yet another jab at Betty, in some ways the worst one so far. They had gone to Indiana for a reunion with the whole Broderick clan at Notre Dame. All five Broderick boys and their father were graduates of the school, and the weekend of college football was an annual event for the family.

It was also the big game against USC, the twenty-fourth anniversary of the weekend Dan and Betty first met and the dream of "happily ever after" seemed a sure thing.

8

LOST WEEKEND

L IKE MILLIONS OF OTHER WOMEN, ELISABETH ANNE BRODERICK FACED A future far different from the one she had once envisioned. Unlike most of those other women, Betty didn't adjust to the loss of her dreams and the destruction of her world.

Dan's departure and eventual divorce left Betty on her own, watching someone else reap the benefits of her hard work. In the rather restricted suburban world of La Jolla, a divorced woman was cut off from much of her former life. Country club memberships are usually in a man's name. Charity organizations prefer volunteers with a steadily increasing income and an expanding list of social contacts.

Betty's adult life had been focused on Dan's career; her friends were mostly the wives of lawyers or the mothers of her children's classmates. Her identity had been built on her marriage. She was Mrs. Daniel T. Broderick III, wife of the young, ambitious, and successful medical malpractice attorney who was tearing up the legal community.

And then it all ended.

She no longer had entrée to either of those familiar worlds. Another ex-wife of an attorney didn't carry much weight. A mother who didn't have custody of her children had even less. Well-meaning advice to put the past behind her and get on with her future must have seemed especially inane to Betty, who could see around her the legally sanctioned wreckage of the only life she wanted or imagined.

The law and the courts were Dan's place, and Betty didn't even try to understand them. Somewhat like a husband who escapes from helping with the dishes by dropping them when he dries, Betty wanted out of the legal system by breaking its rules and smashing its conventions. An educated, witty woman who charmed even her antagonists, she professed total ignorance of legal terms and regularly exaggerated the language and the consequences of the warnings and decisions she always seemed to be getting.

Melanie Cohrs remembered once finding Betty nearly frantic over legal documents that she had received that day. She was going to be sent back to jail, she said. Hoping to calm her, Cohrs invited Betty to spend the night at her house, and as they packed an overnight bag, she glanced at the papers that had so upset her friend.

"It didn't have anything to do with her going to jail," Cohrs testified. The papers that she read were about Betty using obscenities on the answering machine messages. Cohrs said after that incident, she became concerned about how much Betty understood of the legal maneuvering she was part of.

To those who remember that most of the civil laws in the United States are based on British common law—a system developed by the medieval robber barons to protect themselves against incursions by their equals—there was a particular irony about the Broderick divorce.

Women who suffer physical abuse often strike back when their tormentor is drunk or asleep. Their actions are not considered self-defense, as defined by those armor-wearing fighters of long ago. Attorneys who have represented battered women in such cases are working to change the laws, or at least the legal understanding of what constitutes a fair fight when the opponents are of unequal strength and skill.

Instead of the chivalry of a knight rescuing a damsel in distress, Dan Broderick often exhibited the callousness of a dragon devouring whatever tidbit fell in his path. He used his skill and talents and experience to keep Betty off-balance and under pressure. Friends and colleagues argue Dan could have been a lot tougher on Betty in court, given her propensity for trespassing in his home and leaving obscene messages on his phone.

But nineteen years and nine pregnancies together ought to mean something more than just following the depersonalized rules of the courts and the system. Betty's longest-standing complaint against Dan was his coldness, and it would continue to be a source of deep bitterness to her. She could never bring herself to believe that the man who had shared her bed for so many years would not even speak to her again.

In many ways, Betty had been hit as hard as a woman who was suddenly widowed. The man that she had married and grown up with no longer existed. Dan Broderick was still there, but he bore no resemblance to the ambitious medical student in a tiny dorm room or to the struggling law student coming home with his Portuguese neighbors or even to the youthful father who had shared the joys of their babies and the pain of losing so many others.

That man, the one who courted her for three years, would not have refused to speak to her. He would have understood how angry Betty was about the betrayal of her dreams, the broken promises of the wedding vows, and the abandonment of the life they had built together. Nor would he have taunted her with being "crazy" in the face of her very serious emotional problems.

The nonstop legal proceedings were very much in character, however.

In the three years since Dan Broderick had first filed for divorce, he had brought nearly two dozen harassment charges against Betty. In addition, there were motion papers filed about custody, alimony, community property, court hearings, judgments, depositions, and a myriad and one other things. The amassed documents eventually filled nine files, stacked almost a foot high and weighing nearly twenty pounds.

"Every single time I was served, I felt like I was being attacked," Betty Broderick testified. When they were still married, Dan would gloat about his method of litigation, overwhelming his opponent with motions and countermotions until he won a settlement just to end the paperwork.

Betty was sure Dan was doing the same thing to her. If she agreed to one demand, he would come to court with another one. She saw no escape from an unequal battle in an arena that favored her opponent. Her fears, real and imagined, gave her sleepless nights and anxiety-ridden days.

"At home alone in my house with no one to speak to and this omnipresent pile of legal stuff coming at me all the time, I would get very upset about my personal situation," Betty recalled. Her frustration and sense of helplessness would be overwhelming at times. She remembered "a lot of times" that she would get dressed to go out for the evening and be unable to leave her house.

"I was so upset and so depressed I just couldn't go places and pretend," she explained, adding that she didn't feel she could mask her anxieties about her future. "You know, cocktail talk, everything's fine and everything's rosy."

At the end of October in 1989 Betty seemed to be doing better. The hearings at the start of the year had produced a final ruling in March, giving her alimony of $16,100 a month, dividing the community property, and awarding Dan custody of the two boys, but Betty had hired a new lawyer to fight that.

She was upset when she heard that Linda had accompanied Dan to Notre Dame for the football weekend reunion of the Broderick clan. It was another of those bedeviling details that seemed like a purposeful campaign against her.

But there were also signs that she was making an attempt to find a new life and new interests. She was excited about an interview for a job that she wanted at a greeting card company. Kim was leaving for school in Arizona, and they had spent some time together that week without quarreling, a welcome change from their often acrimonious meetings.

But as so often happened, at least in Betty's mind, just as she seemed to be getting things under control, something would crop up that involved court appearances and attorney's fees and more pieces of paper filled with the long words, redundant phrases, and arcane clauses favored by the legal profession.

As the weekend began, Betty had a call from Kim in Tucson. It was the kind of call thousands of parents get from college every week—a request for money. Betty's alimony, drained by her legal fees and personal bills, didn't include spending money for Kim, but she promised to try to help.

Worried by her financial problems—she now had to meet bank loans on both the house and the new condo—Betty went for one of her frequent early morning walks on the beach that Friday. She ran into Kim's old boyfriend, Paul Hathaway, who later remembered Betty as being "one pissed-off lady" who was furious with Dan Broderick. He testified that she said that she "could kill the son of a bitch," then he added that she had made similar threats at other times and he didn't take them seriously.

When she returned home, another reminder of her uncertain situation came in the mail. Just looking at it made Betty nervous. She tried to put it in the back of her mind as she prepared for a shopping expedition with her daughter Lee. Nordstrom's was having a half-yearly sale.

When Lee arrived, Betty mentioned the thick letter that had arrived from her lawyer and how upset she was, but her younger daughter brushed those concerns aside. She reassured her mother that all would be well and urged her on to the planned shopping trip.

"I didn't want to ask questions," Lee said later. "I knew if I brought it up, it would put her in a bad mood and we'd never end up going shopping."

Lee had watched over the years as her mother's responses became more hysterical and her reactions more erratic with every new setback. Only twelve when Betty burned Dan's clothes in the backyard at Coral Reef, now Lee was nineteen and Betty's gestures had escalated.

For her own protection, the young woman had learned to avoid the topics that would bring on her mother's anger or allow her to voice her unending complaints about the divorce, the legal system, and the two people who she considered had undermined her life, Dan and

Linda. All the Broderick children had learned to duck out of the line of fire whenever open hostilities broke out between their parents.

Lee's distraction worked, and the shopping trip to Nordstrom's went without incident. Lee and Betty parted to pursue their separate plans for the rest of the weekend. It seemed much like so many others in the past few years.

Danny and Rhett were spending the time with Betty. So was Brad Wright. The boys had a soccer game scheduled on Saturday, and she planned to take them for haircuts, but she had time to chat when Helen Pickard stopped by in the morning.

Pickard remembered Betty's house was almost empty of furniture that day because she was in the middle of moving to the condo. But Helen had a cup of coffee and a bagel and stayed chatting for nearly an hour.

As usual, Betty talked about her legal problems and told Pickard that she had received another letter just the day before, again threatening to put her in jail. A carefully coiffed and made-up woman in middle-age, Pickard said disdainfully that she didn't look at Betty's private papers lying on the mantelpiece and couldn't be sure that's what the letter said.

Saturday passed as planned. Betty went grocery shopping, stocking up on necessities and delicacies like veal and swordfish, spending she estimated nearly $400. Then, chronically short of sleep, she lay down briefly after dinner and fell asleep fully dressed. At some point her youngest son, Rhett, crawled into bed with her. She recalled waking up several times during the night, but that happened often.

Awake again before dawn, she considered taking a shower, but worried that the sound of running water would wake up Rhett. Going into the kitchen to make coffee, Betty noticed the lawyer's letter and its enclosed papers, now on the counter. She read it for the first time and felt again the familiar sense of panic and anxiety.

"The letter said to me . . . you're going to jail," Betty testified two years later. "You're going to be fined . . . Linda's going to screw around with the machine again and keep you from your sons . . . You're going to play her games again and drive you crazy and that's why she's doing it, to create contempt orders."

To Betty, the letter seemed to assure another delay. It was already November, and custody of the boys was supposed to have been settled before school began. Betty had promised them it would be over soon. Now it looked like everything was starting up all over again.

Danny, now thirteen, was an adolescent and already too blasé to get involved in the holiday celebrations that Betty liked so much. She felt as if she was missing out on all the wondrous moments of childhood that could never be recaptured. More hearings meant more legal fees and court appearances and another year gone without a decision.

"I'd promised them by September, they'd be living with me," Betty recalled of her feelings on that morning. "I promised and promised. I was unable to live up to my promises so many times. On this day I felt I'd absolutely failed those kids.

"I could not get them. I'd tried and tried . . . and I wasn't going to get them . . . We were going to play this game instead . . . The kids were going to be very disappointed in me."

In the dim light of that predawn morning, Betty saw only menacing shadows and intimidating outlines, further threatening the peace and happiness of her children and herself. The boys wanted to live with her, but Dan had custody and would restrict their visits to her as punishment. Lee had been disowned entirely. And Kim had called over the weekend to say she needed money for school, but Dan didn't want to send her any more.

"I had been beaten down for so long, so many times," Betty said. "I felt that all the resources a person draws on when they're in trouble, that I had over the years exhausted all those resources . . . It was six years into this."

Her birthday was only a few days away, her forty-second. The troubles had begun in 1983, and she felt as if the years in between had been wasted—"I hadn't been able to get a job or make a decision about where I'm living and help my kids or do anything."

Her family back in New York seemed to have lost patience years earlier. Betty's parents were reportedly visiting her when the Coral Reef house was sold and she rammed her car into Dan's door. They left after she was hospitalized. When *Los Angeles Times* reporter Amy

Wallace went to talk with Betty's parents after her arrest, Mrs. Bisceglia refused to talk to the writer, saying only, "We are a couple in our mid-seventies and we are hanging on by our fingernails to get through this . . . We have nothing to say."

Friends, too, had long since grown tired of listening to Betty's complaints and angry diatribes. Most had urged her many times to seek therapy, to put her rage away, to find a new direction for her life. She would try to follow the advice, then she'd get caught up in another court fight and the emotions it evoked.

It's difficult to start a new life when you never wanted the old one to end. Like anyone faced with an unexpected loss, Betty tried to find a reason for the sudden turn her life had taken. In her case, the cause seemed obvious. Dan's actions had changed her life totally.

This newest letter seemed to again shake the foundations she was trying to build. It carried the suggested threat of fines at a time when her finances were more precarious than ever. She was trying to sell her house, but until she did, she was paying monthly charges on both it and the condominium. Her credit card debt was nearly $50,000, and she owed nearly ten times that much in legal fees connected with the divorce. Now there would be more.

She recalled her thinking in those early morning hours: "I just cannot be reduced back to the fines and the court and the threats and the contempts and just pull the money out and watch her go crazy and watch everything fall apart . . .

"Why can't they just leave me alone to get control of my life and get my kids and have a peaceful, normal life . . . I didn't know what kind of sick jollies they were getting out of driving me crazy . . ."

Sitting at her kitchen counter, she tried to write a response to the latest letter from Kathleen Cuffaro, one of Dan's new associates who was handling the divorce motions. Betty's attempt at a businesslike tone was a failure and her thoughts were getting more depressed.

On the wall near by was a Holy Card saying, "God will not give you more than you can handle." The words had comforted Betty in the past, giving her strength when she thought she had no more. It reminded her of the motto—"One day at a time"—for Al-ANON, the support group for people living with addicted personalities. But this time the words of the card didn't comfort her, and the wisdom of not worrying about tomorrow failed to calm her overwrought emotions.

"I looked at the card and thought, 'I can't handle it,'" Betty recalled. "The card is not helping me. This is more than I can handle."

Desperate and upset—"under a lot of pressure from a million different places"—Betty started to write a suicide note, beginning with the words "I can't take this anymore." She listed three things that she said had driven her to contemplate taking her own life. Two years later her voice broke as she read her reasons from the witness stand at her murder trial:

> "One, Linda Kolkena, the cunt, interfering with what little contact I have left with my chilldren. She's been doing it for years. We've litigated it continuously.
>
> Two, the constant threats of court, jail, contempt, fines, etcetera which is very scary to me, and no matter what the evidence, I always lose.
>
> Three, them constantly insinuating I'm crazy."

As she reread the letter she wrote in those early morning hours, the emotions she felt then seemed to come flooding back. Betty began crying as she told the court that "the last sentence of this letter says that 'her emotional disturbance and mental disease . . . ' That was the same thing he'd been telling me since 1983," the sobbing woman recounted, "that I'm emotionally disturbed and I have a mental disease. It was never that. I couldn't stand getting attacked like this."

That November day, hoping to calm her turbulent thoughts and gain some perspective, Betty decided to make a predawn visit to the beach. One of the advantages of living in La Jolla was the easy access to miles of sandy shores and pounding surf.

Most mornings, Betty made her way to the Pacific, usually stopping at a nearby convenience store for a cup of half coffee and half cocoa to sip as she walked and watched the waves.

"When you feel how I felt, you hyperventilate," she explained. "I feel like I can't get a breath. I go to the beach because of all the air, just to make yourself feel better. [I would] walk along or sit on the beach, but basically to get air."

Her mood changed, she recalled, as she drove to the shore. The fears and frustrations of the past few years kept running through her mind. "What the hell do I have that they want now?" she remembered wondering. "The only answer I could come up with is that they wanted to drive me crazy. It was sadistic, what they were doing."

Again Betty thought about killing herself. Several entries in her diary had contained passages that discussed suicide. But she was determined to do it in a way that would make even Dan recognize his responsibility.

"I can't do this anymore," she remembered thinking. "I can't go to court anymore, I can't go to jail anymore. I want to end it. I had to make it stop, or I was going to kill myself.

"I was just going to kill myself in his house, not down at the beach, not at my house," she said later. "I wanted to kill myself right in front of him and splash my brains all over his goddamned house . . . I'd been contemplating suicide for a long time . . ."

Somewhere along the short drive to the beach, she turned around and headed for Marston Hills. She had a new plan, to confront Dan Broderick one more time, asking for custody of the two boys. If he still refused her demands, Betty intended to kill herself.

"I knew if I killed myself it was going to be in front of Dan Broderick," Betty explained in court. " . . . so that everyone would know that's why, that I wasn't crazy . . . He wanted me to kill myself so that he could go on living and say, 'See, I told you all she was just a nut. She was just crazy.' "

To guarantee that he would talk to her, and to carry out the last piece of her plan if necessary, she had the .38-caliber revolver hidden in her purse. Going to Dan's house early in the morning would be a surprise and make it more difficult for him to call the police and have her arrested for violating the restraining order.

"I brought the gun with me initially in order to make them have to talk to me," she said in court. "If they said they were calling the police I'd say, 'No you're not.' If he wouldn't deal with me, give me the kids, I was just going to kill myself."

She also had an unexpected advantage. On the front seat of the Suburban was a box of miscellaneous junk on its way from the house to the condo. On top was a key ring including one very odd-looking large key. Betty remembered her children laughing about the "funny looking" key to Dan Broderick's new house.

Kim had recently lost her key ring, with Dan's key on it. This key ring had turned up in Betty's house. The odds seemed good that the strange-looking key would open the doors to the house on Cypress Avenue. If not, there would be another way in. She had always managed to get inside before.

Betty Broderick testified that she didn't remember much about the drive from La Jolla to Marston Hills. Her thoughts were disorganized, "churning in my head," and she wasn't even aware of what road she took.

"I've got to make this stop, I've got to make this stop," she remembered thinking over and over.

As she described her feelings later in court, her hands, one clutching a white handkerchief, flew in circles in front of her face or flailed off to one side. Her voice would break and she would start to cry as she tried to re-create the emotions that she had felt on that Sunday morning.

"There was so much going on inside my head, like my eyeballs were turned backwards," Betty remembered. "The whole world was inside my head because of all this anguish, so I wasn't seeing where I was going.

"It felt like I was in Hell, actually."

9

GONE WITH THE WIND

NOBODY LIKES A LOSER, AND BETTY BRODERICK WAS A LOSER, BIG-TIME. She lost her children, her home, and her husband. She no longer had a social position. She had lost her dignity and her temper. She lost control altogether for a few brief seconds, and then she lost her freedom. She was about to lose any shred of privacy she may have hoped to cling to.

Twelve hours after the five shots shattered the silence of Marston Hills, Betty Broderick, accompanied by attorney Ronald Frant, turned herself in to the San Diego police. She was placed on a suicide watch at the woman's jail in Santee and recalled, "I was stark naked for the first night I was there . . . I was real shocky and I don't remember much of what happened . . . I just went where people told me to go."

If the first part of Betty Broderick's life was a fairy tale, and the last few years had been a cliché, the next phase would be a nightmare.

The death of Linda and Dan Broderick and the arrest of his ex-wife made front-page headlines. Long background articles provided the messy history of the Broderick divorce and Betty's complaints about unfair treatment. The first story in the *San Diego Tribune*, the afternoon paper, also quoted from friends of Dan's and Linda's, grief-stricken and outraged.

Betty had broken the taboo against women reacting violently in anger. The daily newspapers in every major city regularly carry stories about men who have shot, strangled, stabbed or otherwise killed the women who had rejected them. The tale is so common that it rarely rates more than a paragraph or two in the back pages.

But Betty Broderick's case had all the elements of a Hollywood movie and made great newspaper stories. There was jealousy, murder, betrayal, greed, and Betty's bizarre earlier behavior to add color. Further, the main characters were all photogenic, well-educated, upper-middle-class suburbanites, the kind of people who didn't do things like this.

The immediate reaction of Dan's friends and colleagues to the horror of his death was to portray him as the victim of a crazed woman who had made his life miserable. Even that first story told of Betty's vocal and frequent threats, the armed guards that Dan had hired for his wedding only months earlier, the harassment charges sustained in court, and her demands for more money despite the already high alimony payments.

Without effort or planning, the picture was already visible in outline—a jealous, obsessive, greedy woman who had refused to allow her ex-husband any peace or happiness with a new wife. It was a familiar picture.

Women who take action against their tormentors are almost always viewed as harridans, nags, harpies, witches, or other undesirable female extremes. In contrast, a man accused of killing an unfaithful mate or even a rejecting girlfriend is portrayed as defending his honor or acting in the heat of passion.

Defense attorney Jack Earley recalled that one of the first successful insanity pleas in the United States was an eighteenth-century murder case that involved the sheriff of Washington, D.C., who looked out a second-story window and spotted his wife walking down the street with another man. He went downstairs and killed the other man. At his trial the sheriff pleaded not guilty by reason of insanity—

the sight of his wife with another man had made him crazy with jealousy. He was acquitted.

Until recently in some third-world countries, men who murdered a betraying mate were not even tried. Such savage responses were expected, even required, of a man, and often excused. Women who responded with violence when faced with betrayal and lies were the exception, and were usually severely punished as an example and a warning to other women. They still are.

In the macho world of San Diego, Betty was every man's worst nightmare. She didn't sit quietly while Dan cavorted publicly with Linda. She had broadcast her complaints about her treatment in the courts to anyone who would listen. She had hinted to everyone she could reach of a conspiracy by those entrusted with the justice system. When that didn't help, she took the action she believed necessary to put a stop to what she saw as the cause of the unhappiness in her life.

The bloody aftermath of her action left the city in a state of shock. As one Marston Hills neighbor commented to the *San Diego Tribune,* "This is a very, very quiet area . . . It's the first time I've seen two bodies wrapped in blankets come out on stretchers on this block."

The first stories, built on interviews with the friends of both Dan's and Betty's, broadly outlined the pair's history, including the recent disputes over custody and alimony. Members of HALT talked about Betty's complaints against Dan, while his colleagues and associates described his legal abilities and his reputation.

One of the very first articles contained the story of Dan's 1988 proposal on one knee in the middle of Dobson's Restaurant, describing Linda as a paralegal who worked for him without alluding to their long-standing affair. The writer also commented on Dan's "low-key" lifestyle, referring to him as a millionaire lawyer who lived in Hillcrest, the middle-class neighborhood on the other side of the Cabrillo Freeway. Apparently unaware that the residents of Cypress Avenue identified their neighborhood as Marston Hills, the reporter also seemed ignorant of the top hat, cape, custom suits, and sporty cars that made up the more flamboyant aspects of the Broderick persona.

Dan was described as "a credit to the bar and a credit to the practice" by one rival, and a "down-to-earth swell guy" by a former city aide. His friends talked about how Betty had harassed him, forcing Dan to hire an armed guard for his wedding. Gerald Barry, Jr., his divorce attorney, said that Dan had refused to take further precautions against his ex-wife because "he did not want to live his life looking over his shoulder."

The underlying theme was Betty's overwhelming greed and obsessive jealousy against Dan's saintly patience and courageous demeanor. Even the details, repeated endlessly, reinforced those impressions. Beginning with the early news stories and throughout the next two years, Betty was identified as "a La Jolla socialite," although those truly active in the local society doings barely knew her. Still, it was another titillating detail that added to the interest that the case was generating.

"That's always been just the funniest thing in the world, when they call her a socialite," Jack Earley commented after the trials. "She was never a socialite, especially in La Jolla. People laugh, when they hear that, who know what's going on. For the lawyers, they like to paint Betty that way, they like to paint her as a money-hungry woman. That's what the San Diego legal community has painted her and that's what they'll always paint her—as someone only concerned with money."

Kerry Wells thought Betty had a very active social life—"She was involved in a fair amount of social activities, charitable organizations, and she was involved in the Bar Auxiliary"—but agreed the socialite tag was not really appropriate. She said she didn't know how the media got the impression that Betty was a socialite, but blamed it on the frenzy of the case: "Reporters sort of go out and it sort of snowballs."

Much of the emerging picture came from statements issued, usually in response to questions, from the prosecutor. As head of the District Attorney's Family Violence Unit, Kerry Wells was assigned the case from the start. With short, curly red hair and large horn-rimmed glasses, the dimpled Wells resembles a grown-up Orphan Annie. In one of her earliest statements, she opined that Betty might face the death penalty if it was established that the case met the "special circumstances" criteria the state of California requires for a capital prosecution.

Eventually, the D.A.'s office decided against a death penalty case. Kerry Wells explained that all four Broderick children would probably be called as witnesses, and to put them "in the position of having to play a part in perhaps losing their mother to the gas chamber is just too much."

A magna cum laude graduate of Whittier Law School, Wells was in her thirties, the married mother of two sons. She had joined the district attorney's office in 1982, working most of the time with victims of abuse. Her job put her in daily contact with battered women left in abject poverty to provide for several small children. Her empathy for Betty Broderick's situation was limited, her disgust for Betty's solution total.

Kerry Wells wasn't alone. No one condoned Betty's actions. A few felt some sympathy for her situation and the circumstances that made her so desperate. But two people were dead, shot in their bedroom on a Sunday morning.

Three days after the murders another article appeared, based on police affidavits and interviews with Dan's friends and colleagues. The official statements portray Elisabeth Broderick as a woman dangerous to everyone around her: "Indications were that she made numerous threats to kill [Dan] in the past. She also threatened to kill Linda as well."

The outrage of those who knew Dan and Linda was apparent, and most made no effort to disguise the emotions raised by the manner of his death. Bonnie Reading, the lawyer who had sent Betty to see Daniel Jaffe, commented that although Dan Broderick could have afforded private guards and special security devices to ward off Betty's harassment, he had "decided not to let her craziness drive his life."

The incumbent president of the San Diego Bar Association foresaw a potential defense move and tried to head it off. Marc Adelman announced that he didn't think it was a good idea for other lawyers to talk to reporters about the Broderick divorce and its long-standing problems because "we want to assure that the trial is held in this county. I'd hate to see an insanity defense tried in Eureka . . . or San Francisco."

The article, in the *Los Angeles Times* San Diego edition, pointed out that Family Court had had metal detectors long before the city's other courts because "that's where the most violence occurred." It was a rather oblique way of pointing out that Betty Broderick was not the first person driven to brutality by emotions that originated in the home.

One of the lawyers who worked for Dan, Robert Vaage, told police that Betty's ownership of a gun was well known and that "she was capable of carrying out her threats." His statement even suggested a motive: "It was common knowledge Dan and Linda were thinking of starting a family of their own. This made Betty real upset because she figured Linda was getting everything. I know Betty was also upset because Dan and Linda were thinking of buying a home in Utah."

Betty's friends were also interviewed by the *Times*, and they tried to present her side of the past few years. One woman, who refused to be identified, talked about Betty's long-standing frustration over the divorce and custody proceedings with reporter Amy Wallace:

"[Betty] became more emotional, which was interpreted as instability. In a sense it was a long-term kind of Chinese torture. It just drove her crazy. She was really just so fried that the legal system had done her in and that a person can control your life from outside and nobody would ever know."

Other friends talked to reporters about her love of children and devotion to being a mother, describing her as a "car-pool-type mom" who baked and cooked special treats when she was expecting her children for the weekend. They managed to lighten the black portrait being painted by Dan's and Linda's families, friends and colleagues, although Frant warned Betty's supporters not to discuss the specifics of the case.

The attorney first met Betty with Dian Black on that Sunday afternoon before her surrender. He was at her side in court three days later, asking for a delay of her arraignment, but told reporters later that he was not her trial attorney. Betty, dressed in light blue jail clothes and waist chains, told the judge herself that she agreed to the delay and waived her right to a bail hearing at the time. Kim and Lee, both present in the courtroom, sobbed when they saw their mother.

There were more tears, of course, on Friday, November 10, when a memorial service was held for Dan and Linda in St. Joseph's Cathedral. Hundreds of friends and colleagues, including a federal district judge, joined the Brodericks and Kolkenas to eulogize the pair at the downtown church. Red roses covered Dan's wooden coffin and white ones blanketed Linda's matching one. All four children were present; one of the girls broke down on the steps of the church. The younger Broderick boys looked "anguished" to at least one observer.

Betty would later complain because she was not allowed to attend the funeral, adding in her opinion the whole thing was badly handled.

Even more frustrating for her, Danny and Rhett were gone, taken out of California to live with Dan's brother Larry and his wife Kathy in Colorado. Betty was not allowed to see or speak to the boys before they left, nor to write them letters or even send birthday cards afterward.

It was the first sign that the family Betty wanted so much to bring back together had been irrevocably destroyed, but it would be a long time before she recognized or even understood that. She continued to talk and plan as if she had not been responsible for the enormous loss she imposed on her four children. There were other signs that the immensity of her actions had not yet registered.

Over the weekend after the funeral, Betty found a new lawyer. Frant had been replaced by Mark Wolf, a highly regarded local criminal defense attorney who had "never ever" met Dan Broderick. He was in court when Betty, this time dressed in her own clothes—a stylish beige blouse and slacks—pleaded not guilty. Talking with reporters after Betty's arraignment, Wolf said his client understood the charges against her, but seemed to be somewhat out of touch with reality.

"She uses the present tense when she talks about [Dan]," Wolf remarked. "It's as if I talked about my grandfather, who's passed away, and still spoke of him as being alive." The attorney said he didn't correct Betty when she did that because "I'm afraid to. My concern is that I don't want to push her any further than she's already been pushed."

He added that "sometimes she responds appropriately, sometimes she doesn't" to questions and conversation around her.

He wouldn't rule out the possibility of an insanity defense, adding, "It's a very tragic case for everyone involved. It's very clear that that kind of behavior is not sane. But I'm in no position at this point to make any other statements about the strategy in the case."

Aware of the opinions already being heard in the back hallways of the courthouse, Wolf also raised the issue of a fair trial for Betty Broderick in San Diego:

> "I think that there may be thirteen or fourteen people out there who can be fair jurors . . . The problem in this case is going to be finding a judge who can be fair . . . I think you will find there's a great deal of prejudice in the legal community . . . I'm glad that citizens, individual people, and not attorneys make these kinds of decisions."

By then the *San Diego Reader*'s long article on the Broderick divorce, based on the eighteen-month-old interviews with Dan and Betty, had been published. The television tabloid shows were also hot on the story of the rejected wife who had killed her rival and her ex-husband, a prominent attorney.

Wolf, getting dozens of calls from the media and sacks of letters expressing support for or outrage at Betty, retained a public relations firm to handle the demands on his time and to counter some of the negative publicity. That proved to be a mistake that would haunt Betty for the next two years. The prosecution referred to the PR firm at every opportunity, as proof of the defendant's penchant for telling her version of events to anyone who would listen.

At a bail hearing at the end of November, Kerry Wells described Betty as an "absolutely uncontrolled and angry woman" whose release would pose "a significant threat to the rest of this community." She presented letters from Dan's brother Larry and a statement from

Kim—"she indicated that her mother has had an extremely unpredictable personality"—voicing concerns about their safety if Betty got out on bail. She didn't.

Wolf maintained that his client was still having trouble understanding her situation. "She's not really acclimated herself to what's going on in these proceedings," he told reporters outside the courtroom.

She was adjusting to life at Las Colinas, apparently. Betty's friend Helen Pickard recalled in court that she received a call from Betty in jail at Thanksgiving. "She said she'd never been happier, and she acted like it . . . Her voice was exuberant and she sounded great."

Other evidence surfaced later that indicated that sometimes Betty was very aware of what she had done, if not too clear on why or what was going to happen next. Months afterward Kim recalled in court the meeting with her mother a few days after the murders that had so frightened her:

> "It was a bad conversation. Everything was fine at first. [Then] she started to say she had no choice, she couldn't let him do what he was doing. She needed me to support her . . . she'd be out soon . . . I told her I didn't agree with her, and she got mad at me and started yelling, calling me a 'traitor' . . . I don't remember everything she called me."

Alienated and afraid of her mother, Kim soon left San Diego for Colorado. She moved near her younger brothers, leaving Lee behind as the only Broderick sibling still able to see and talk to Betty. Kim eventually resumed a relationship with her mother by long distance when Betty phoned to see how her sons were doing.

Prosecutor Kerry Wells found Betty's actions toward the children personally baffling. "I can understand people going through a bad time, and I can understand people being real upset and having a flash of some sort of physical, violent response," Wells remarked, "but that's not what Elisabeth Broderick did in relation to her children."

In an interview after the case was over, the prosecutor expressed sympathy for the situation Elisabeth Broderick had found herself in when Dan moved out. Wells seemed to think Betty should have gone from June Cleaver to Rosie O'Neill, the middle-aged TV lawyer who gets over her ex-husband's desertion by working in a public defender's office.

"[Betty] was college educated," Wells pointed out. "She was bright; she had a very good personality; she had the ability to do so much. That's the tragedy, I think. She had so much going for her . . . She could have gone to law school and come back and kicked Dan Broderick's butt in court."

Maybe she would have challenged his will, filed in Family Court shortly after the funeral. As he had promised, Lee had been disinherited in an amendment written in August 1988. It said: "I specifically make no provision in this will for my daughter, Lee Gordon Broderick." His estate was to be divided equally among his three remaining children in trust funds, with each getting half the principal at age twenty-five and the other half five years later. Betty was not mentioned.

The details of the long divorce were now the subject of everyone's attention. The attorneys representing the local news media joined the lawyers on both sides in asking that the Broderick divorce file be unsealed. In fact, most of the local legal profession seemed to be in the courtroom for that hearing. Lawyers were there representing the estate, the children, the various media outlets, the D.A., and Betty's criminal and civil cases.

The various requests to unseal the file were denied. The judge cited the potential damage to the children, describing them as "extremely helpless and vulnerable in this situation." Over the objections of the defense, a gag order was slapped on everyone, forbidding any discussion of the case with reporters. It was soon lifted, although Judge H. Ronald Domnitz warned that could change again.

Pointing to what he called "a firestorm of media activity endorsed by [Broderick] or her attorney," the judge said he would restore the order if he became aware of "any further attempt to try this case in the media." Mark Wolf didn't have too much to say after that anyway.

Betty was again hunting for an attorney, apparently angry that Wolf

Betty and Dan Broderick at a lawyer's dinner in 1983.

Dan Broderick and Linda Kolkena at a lawyer's dance in 1987.

(Spencer Busby)

Dan Broderick and Linda Kolkena Broderick at a less formal
gathering after their marriage in April 1988.

The front of Dan Broderick's Southern-style house on Cypress Avenue. The gates were added by another owner.

The rear of the Cypress Avenue house, showing the gully where Kim Broderick hid when her mother rammed her car into the front door in February 1986.

Prosecuting attorney Kerry Wells showing the jury a Broderick family photo in which Dan Broderick's face has been crossed out.

Defense lawyer Jack Early who defended Betty Broderick in both murder trials.

Housekeeper Robin Tu'ua who testified about Betty Broderick's intrusions at the house on Cypress Avenue.

Helen Pickard, a friend of Betty's, who told the jury about her extravagant spending habits and lack of remorse after the deaths of Dan and Linda.

Kim Broderick, Dan and Betty's oldest child, recalled the frequent arguments between her parents, blaming her mother's increasingly bizarre behavior.

Betty Broderick posed for photos before her second trial.

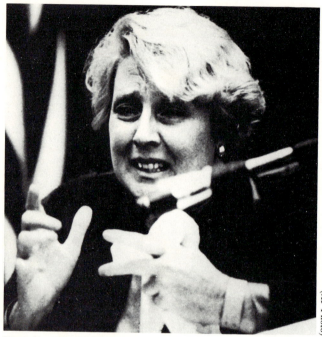

(AP Photo)

Betty Broderick's emotional anguish showed on her face as she
described the years of her marriage, the stress of her drawn-out
divorce, and the morning she shot Dan and Linda.

had hired the public relations firm. After a couple of meetings at the women's jail, she retained an out-of-town lawyer, Jack Earley. Based in Newport Beach, just down the coast from Los Angeles, Earley specialized in homicide cases and found Betty's situation "fairly compelling."

For his part, Mark Wolf held no grudges and continued to speak in Betty's defense. He told reporters that Betty felt "there isn't anybody in San Diego who would be able to take on the bench and the bar in San Diego . . . [and] I can understand that feeling."

He suggested further that Betty's attitude was not misplaced, saying that in less than two months he had already uncovered information that would be "very embarrassing" to the local legal community. "Dan took her to the cleaners, and most of the legal system helped him do that . . . There is very little different in this case than in a battered wife case. The only difference is [that] the two-by-four that Dan Broderick used was the legal system."

Jack Earley agreed with his predecessor. He pointed out that most of Dan's friends, lawyers all, had not been entirely truthful in their earliest statements to the police when they denied any knowledge of an affair between Dan and Linda Kolkena. After the trials, Earley charged angrily that none of these men were called to testify because those first comments made them susceptible to perjury accusations.

A graduate of Loyola Law School, Earley's dark-framed glasses and conservative suits suggest a mild-mannered man who doesn't often become incensed. He seems to have little of the arrogance so prevalent among members of the criminal defense bar. Perhaps his nearly ten years as a public defender in Riverside and Orange counties made him more humble. He opened his own practice in 1982. Since then he had represented almost two dozen homicide clients.

The defense attorney emphasized that he took the case because he was interested in Betty's story and thought she had been badly treated by Dan Broderick during the divorce proceedings. But he said he didn't necessarily buy her theory that the local legal community was involved:

"I started out believing that a lot of it was probably Betty's imagination, but came after a period of time to believe that a large percentage of it was true."

Evidence of Dan's enormous legal clout was the battle that soon developed over the carcass of his law practice. At the time of his death he was reported to have more than two hundred cases pending in state and federal courts. One anonymous client backed up Betty's opinion of Dan as a "killer attorney," saying, "I went to Dan Broderick because I was told he was the guy you don't want to see come through the room from the other side."

Most of the pending cases moved with Broderick associate Robert Vaage to the firm of Thorsnes, Bartolotta, McGuire and Padilla. A few others followed Dan's other associate, Kathleen Cuffaro, who had joined Virginia Nelson, also a medical malpractice specialist and the new president of the San Diego County Bar Association.

Still to be determined was the monetary value of those cases for the purpose of deciding the worth of Dan Broderick's estate. That would take some time because most malpractice cases only acquired real worth once they were settled. The winning attorney got a percentage of the award; Dan's share would be dependent on his contribution to the victory and the amount. His old law firm—Gray, Cary, Ames & Frye—represented the estate in the person of Brian Forbes, also a witness for the prosecution.

Further proof that Betty had been declared persona non grata among the powerful lawyers of San Diego came when Earley began his investigations. Potential witnesses, especially spouses and secretaries of attorneys and judges, refused to testify to things they had seen because it might affect their own futures. Earley said one potential witness was abused when the lawyer spouse learned about the meeting with the defense and became concerned about the impression that would create with colleagues.

It seemed obvious to Jack Earley, removed from the pressures of the local legal community, that the general feeling in San Diego compromised Betty's right to a fair trial. He became convinced that Dan Broderick had hidden much of the joint assets that had accumulated during his marriage to Betty with his brother's corporations in Colorado. Earley felt that Dan had cheated her, managing to avoid accounting for that money in the divorce settlement.

If the odds could be manipulated against Betty in a fairly straightforward divorce proceeding, a criminal trial posed a much more serious threat. She couldn't afford to be a loser there.

10

(In)Admissible Evidence

APPARENTLY BELIEVING THE BEST DEFENSE IS A GOOD OFFENSE, JACK Earley attacked in early March, ten days before a scheduled pretrial hearing.

He filed a motion asking that the entire San Diego County district attorney's office be taken off the case. He argued that the prosecutors had interviewed Betty's divorce attorneys without her permission. Any confidential conversations revealed in the questioning therefore fell under the attorney-client privilege, which she had not waived and which now applied to everyone in the prosecutor's office.

Moving quickly, Earley also tried to bar all the local judges from hearing the case, pointing out that at least several presiding in Family Court were potential witnesses and the rest would be influenced by Daniel Broderick's standing in the "close-knit" legal community of San Diego.

The preliminary hearing made more details of the prosecution's case public. Lee Broderick and Dian Black testified about what Betty had said and done after the shootings. Black remembered Betty saying that she had heard Dan "gurgling in his own blood," and Kerry

Wells called another friend who also recalled Betty saying she had shot Dan that Sunday morning.

Both the defense arguments were rejected. Municipal Court judge Jesus Rodriguez ruled that there had not been enough evidence to prove "that every judge of the San Diego Superior Court is actually biased or prejudiced against defendant or for that matter even had any relationship whatsoever" with Dan Broderick.

Jack Earley threatened to delay the start of the trial by appealing those decisions to higher courts. As a compromise, Judge Rodriguez agreed to a move to Vista, in the northern half of the county. Within a month, however, the case was back in a downtown courtroom at Earley's request.

The defense attorney decided the jury pool in the southern half of the county, especially including La Jolla, would be more understanding of Betty's lifestyle and alimony demands. The more accessible location was convenient for the witnesses but added several miles to Earley's own commute. Earley was driving down from Newport Beach regularly, either to interview witnesses in San Diego or to visit Betty. She had been turned down at another bail hearing in February and was still at Las Colinas, the women's prison in Santee, one of the newer towns in the center of the county.

Santee was only a few miles from La Jolla, but the atmosphere was completely different. Close to the desert, the town was more suggestive of the old west than the lush flowery landscape Betty was accustomed to. The air was drier and dusty, the colors yellow and brown, compared to the salty wetness and bluish greens of life near the ocean. For someone who had not experienced many restrictions in her life, Betty adjusted to prison quickly.

She found the confinement comforting. She explained tellingly at her trial that she was "happy to be locked in a dark, little, safe room where nobody could get me." It seemed the mother of four wanted the security of the womb. The outside world had proved to be too much for her.

Unexpectedly, Betty made a friend in jail, her cellmate Karen Wilkening. Known locally as the Rolodex Madam, Wilkening was probably the most notorious prisoner at Las Colinas until Betty's arrest, and they were both housed in an isolated unit.

Karen fixed Betty's hair for her court appearances and asked her new friend to store some personal items when she left the county jail to begin serving her sentence in the state prison. Wilkening had turned down requests to testify at Betty's trial from both sides, but the two women continued to correspond with each other.

There would be one other change before the main roles were set for the trial. At the end of June 1990, Thomas Whelan became the third and final judge named to preside over the trial, now scheduled to begin in early September. His thick gray hair swept into a pompadour, Whelan made a very judicial appearance. He spent most of the trial leaning back in his big leather armchair, eyes half closed as he listened to the lawyers asking questions and arguing legal points. He was still breaking in his chair and his robes. He had been sworn in as a judge only six months earlier after twenty years as a prosecutor.

Jack Earley had objected to a previous judge's connections to the district attorney's office, but apparently decided to go with the devil he could see this time.

"There's no guarantee when you go out of county that you're going to get somebody with as good a reputation," Earley said, pointing out that Whelan was widely known as "a very fair, conscientious person." The defense attorney said any further challenges would affect his preparation for the trial.

Besides, the publicity on the case was spreading. "Hard Copy" and "A Current Affair," two nationally syndicated tabloid TV shows, had each devoted segments to the killings. Betty herself had been talking at length with *Los Angeles Times* reporter Amy Wallace almost since her arrest. She would call the writer from the pay phone in the jail.

Wallace got a page-one story in March out of Betty's confession that she had shot Dan and Linda in a "desperate act of self-defense" to free herself from a man who tried "to control me totally."

As she had since the shootings first happened, Betty acknowledged she had been holding the gun, but denied any real responsibility for what had happened: "It always makes me mad when people call them the victims. Me and my kids were the victims. There are two dead people, but there were five victims."

Every *Times* article about the case until Betty took the witness stand referred to that March confession.

The longer, more detailed story Wallace produced—"Till Murder Do Us Part"—graced the cover of the paper's Sunday magazine on the first weekend in June. As a result, the Broderick case now had instant recognition statewide, if not across the country. That would come.

Wallace's long article spilled Broderick family secrets not even the court testimony would elicit. Kim recalled bitterly how Betty was angry that her oldest daughter had asked Linda for help when she needed an abortion. Kim insisted that her mother had gotten back at her by telling her grandparents in Pittsburgh as well as friends in San Diego about her predicament. She reported that Betty had had an abortion when she became pregnant during Dan's last year in law school.

"Mom could never admit that she'd ever have a happy life," Kim told reporter Wallace. "That would be admitting that she could get on with herself and that Dad didn't ruin her life."

Readers also learned that Betty's parents had withdrawn from her troubles. They refused to speak to Wallace and said that they had decided not to come to San Diego for their daughter's trial, although her father did come to court for one day. "It's too off their scope of experience," Betty explained to the writer.

Larry Broderick, calling Betty's actions "a cold, calculated execution," remembered the many threats of divorce she had made in sixteen years of marriage to his brother. Wallace also repeated the stories told by friends of Linda and Dan's: that Betty had told Rhett to stab Linda in the stomach if he loved his mother; that Betty had told both boys that Dan would no longer be their father if Linda had a baby.

Jack Earley thought the publicity had some benefits. He believed that the stories made the potential jurors more aware that this was an enormously complex case. Therefore, he felt, they would be more open to the defense arguments. Further, the thousands of letters of support that Betty received in prison from other women who had been through similar emotional and legal battering were heartening.

From the earliest moments of the case periodic articles appeared relating the opinions of the general public. Sometimes those interviewed were women at La Jolla shops or country clubs; sometimes they were men in a bar; a few reporters used excerpts from the letters sent to Betty or Jack Earley.

Opinions were divided. "Betty Backers" were generally older people who seemed more sympathetic to Betty's frustration and often wondered aloud "What took her so long?" Other divorced women identified with her anger and offered the most understanding of her loss of control. Mostly younger people who found her actions indefensible and inexplicable made up the "Betty Bashers." Everyone agreed that she was guilty of something and should be punished somehow, and everyone expressed sympathy for the four Broderick children caught in the middle.

Almost from the beginning the story of Dan and Betty Broderick attracted pop culture comparisons. Their early life was likened to a TV sitcom, usually "Leave It to Beaver" or perhaps "Father Knows Best." The years of divorce and court battles inevitably were compared to *Kramer v. Kramer* and *War of the Roses*.

After the shooting, one commentator called it a reverse *Fatal Attraction*. Once the trial began, the testimony, televised locally, would be described as a real-life "Divorce Court," more riveting than a soap opera. The dramatic elements of the story apparently made it difficult for people to relate to the principals as feeling human beings.

By the end of June a TV movie on the Broderick shootings was in the works, one of forty potential offers Amy Wallace received after her article appeared.

The news that Wallace could be paid for the circumstances of her life story infuriated Betty. She had already sent the writer a ten-page letter expressing her "frustration" with the holes in her article. And she sent off another handwritten missive in response to a query from Paul Krueger of the *San Diego Reader*. The weekly published her reply at the end of June.

Talking to you is talking to anyone from the media —you are media. I don't want to talk with you. No one can be selling any rights to a story they don't know. *No one* knows this story but me and my children. The legal "abuses" were covered up and "lost" and conducted in sealed courtrooms and files. The other abuses were "behind closed doors" of our home, as most domestic violence cases are.

Amy Wallace is young (24?) never have been married or divorced or had children! The idea that she is selling my story is ludicrous. She has no idea of what went on at all. Our story is not for sale to anybody at any time for any price. We've all been through enough.

Betty did not understand that her life was now in the public domain forever.

Even her diary was grist for the prosecutor's mill. Kerry Wells wanted to see the diaries Betty had been keeping since Dan walked out. They had been in the box of legal papers that Lee had taken from Betty's condo on the morning of the shooting. The prosecutor said that she didn't even know about them until six months later. The defense had been going through them all that time.

Earley argued that his client was "still presumed to be innocent, still a private citizen, and still has a right to privacy to things that she owns." The ten volumes of Betty's writing, including the manuscript for her memoir of her marriage, "What's a Nice Girl to Do? A Story of White Collar Domestic Violence in America," covered three and a half years, from March 1985 to the middle of 1988.

Although they ended more than a year before the shootings, the judge ordered them turned over to the prosecution. "Just as a gun would be evidence of how a homicide was committed, these diaries could be evidence of why," Judge Whelan ruled.

The defense had a list of documents it needed as well. Jack Earley wanted a detailed accounting of the Broderick finances from the early 1980s, including a complete record of checks written to either Larry

Broderick or Linda Kolkena. He, too, was given the papers and files he requested. He also won approval to broaden his client's testimony to include the years of her marriage and divorce.

"This was a case where I told the court and district attorney, Let's just let everyone in the world come in and say what they want to say to the jury," Jack Earley said afterward. "Neither side objects. You can bring in the worst things that anyone has to say about Betty, and you let me bring in all my evidence, and we'll let the jury decide knowing everything in the world."

Earley, hampered by Betty's confession, insisted nevertheless that she was not guilty of the charge of first degree murder and its potential sentence of life without parole. He argued that there had been no premeditation, that Betty was acting in the heat of passion and also in self-defense. The jury would have to know the full history of the Brodericks to understand.

Kerry Wells had contended that if Betty weren't limited to her thoughts and actions at the time of the shooting, she would "verbalize her alleged maltreatment during the years of her marriage ad nauseam." The judge disagreed. He raised some doubts aloud about the self-defense argument, which he defined as "the imminent threat of death or great bodily harm." He also made another limit on the defendant's case, restricting how much information about Dan's character would be allowed to come before the jury.

"I don't know if he's being unfair," Earley said afterward, shaking his head. "I just don't think that he had any understanding of it at all." It was decisions like that which convinced Jack Earley that Betty's experiences in divorce court were not much exaggerated.

"If someone gets to be known as disliked by somebody or a crackpot, you come in with that reputation," Earley said, pointing out that the same thing applies in any professional or social community. "Anything you do is going to hurt you. It doesn't matter whether you are or not. I'm sure that Betty, when she walked into the courtroom, those judges already knew, she's the nut."

Some of the jurors may have been thinking that also. And jury selection was about to begin.

11

ANATOMY OF A MURDER

T HE OLDE ENGLISH COMMON LAW SYSTEM THAT PROVIDED A DEFINITION OF self-defense appropriate to two men wearing armor also demanded a jury of peers to sit in judgment on a defendant; in those early days, "a jury of peers" meant people, defined as men, who knew the person charged with a crime and could make an informed decision about the evidence and circumstances.

Time and complexity changed the original intent. Modern legal practice called for jurors who had had no contact with the individuals involved in the trial and no knowledge of the situation being judged.

In Betty's trial, both sides agreed that it would be nearly impossible to find people in San Diego County who had not heard about the case. Following what had become standard procedure in high-profile criminal cases, a thirty-four-page questionnaire was put together by the two attorneys and the judge to weed out those citizens who had already formed an opinion about her guilt.

Jury selection began in late September with preliminary questions that eliminated about two-thirds of the potential pool, people who said they would suffer time or money hardships during the expected six weeks of the trial. Judge Whelan said "in no event" would it go until Thanksgiving. He was wrong.

More than a hundred people were then asked to respond to 150 questions probing their attitudes on divorce, abortion, obscene language, and lawyers, as well as their knowledge of the case. After three weeks of voir dire questioning, a jury of six men and six women, plus three alternates, was chosen. Opening arguments were scheduled for October 23, 1990, almost one year since the five shots had been fired.

The panel seemed to be a cross-section of the community in its mix of age, gender, occupation, and backgrounds. Three of its members were sixty-one years old. The youngest was a nineteen-year-old woman who worked part-time in a tanning salon. The government employees encompassed two civilians who worked for the Navy, a county pollution inspector, a teacher, a former preschool aide, and a California Transit worker. The other five jurors included a flight attendant, an executive, a building contractor, an industrial project manager, and an employee of Pacific Bell.

In their answers on the questionnaire, released to the press after they were impaneled, they showed a generally high opinion of judges and a low one of newspaper reporters. Several admitted to having had bitter experiences romantically; one acknowledged that he "can't stand" vulgar language from women, while another described the media response to the case as "a circus." They were all about to get front-row seats to what would probably prove to be the most dramatic and most emotional presentation they would ever see, and their ultimate decision as an audience would be more important than any review by a Broadway critic.

The house was packed for the opening arguments—each lawyer's first statement of the case to be proved. Betty Broderick's trial for the murders of Dan and Linda Broderick promised to be the best show in town, and the spectators lined up at 7:15 A.M. to get the few public seats out of the thirty-six in the small courtroom. A TV monitor in the hallway, provided by the local stations taping the testimony, accommodated the nearly one hundred late-comers.

The defendant was prepared for her starring role. She had lost almost thirty pounds, the side effect from an antidepressant prescribed in prison. Betty reportedly became deeply depressed after Lee didn't get to Las Colinas in time for visiting hours on Mother's Day the previous May. But at the time of the trial, the weight loss looked terrific.

Betty's hair didn't look as professionally done as it had during the spring preliminary hearings, because Karen Wilkening had been transferred to state prison, and Betty had to share one set of rollers with other inmates. And at one court appearance she wore a stylish electric-blue suit that appeared to signal bright hopes for the drama and emotions of the days and weeks to come.

A criminal trial falls somewhere between a tragic play and an athletic competition. There are two sides opposing each other, hoping to score points with a group of impartial observers by presenting testimony and evidence in a dramatic way that reveals an ultimate truth. Many lawyers possess histrionic skills that would be as much at home on a stage as a court of law. They plan their tactics and strategy in an effort to make the best advantage of the most emotional and climactic moments. As with any live, unrehearsed performance, there are always surprises—from the other side, and often from your own witnesses as well, no matter how prepared an attorney may be.

Jack Earley and Kerry Wells had done their homework. Both lawyers had spent the better part of the past year preparing for the trial: interviewing witnesses, researching arguments and precedents, learning the details of the medical testimony, and countering evidence from the opposition. The large number of attorneys and people associated with the legal community involved in the case added another layer of complexity to the normal difficulty of preparation for any jury trial. Media queries just contributed to the confusion and pressure.

Earley, who specializes in homicide defenses, had learned to live with local reporters. Kerry Wells was more accustomed to the anonymity of prosecuting domestic violence cases.

"I've never been able to put on a case without feeling in some way emotionally toward the case, and usually, of course, it's toward the victim," Wells said. "You wouldn't be prosecuting the case if you didn't really believe the defendant was guilty, so it's very hard to not think about the possibility that a guilty person might not be convicted. You put a lot of internal pressure on yourself to make sure that the right thing happens."

That she believed deeply in Betty Broderick's guilt was evident from her opening statement: "This case, to put it in the simplest possible terms, is about hate and revenge and murder.

"It's about a woman who had so many things going for her that she could have done so much with—like a million-dollar home in La Jolla, like a sixteen-thousand-dollar-a-month income, like intelligence and education and friends and four beautiful children. But none of it was enough, because she was so consumed with hate."

Kerry Wells insisted that Betty's motivation was money, not love or even hate: "It wasn't the loss of love or the emotional loss that made her so mad. The defendant had said that she was never in love with Daniel Broderick, that she married him because she knew he was going to be a money-maker. She knew that he was going to be a success. And she would be assured of having . . . a privileged life. When the marriage ended and he continued to be a success in his life, she was furious."

Linda Kolkena, Wells said, "had what [Betty] still felt belonged to her and only her and she hated her for it . . . There was no way she was going to let them live happily ever after."

Conceding his client had pulled the trigger, Earley said, "We don't contest the facts," but he insisted the real issue was, "What is her mental state? What is going on? What made her do this?"

The defense attorney's argument offered the jury a portrait of a much different woman: "She was someone who was left without family, children, home—who she was, where she was going. And what you see left is a person who acts."

A large white board mounted on an easel held photos of the Broderick family attached with Velcro; it stood in front of the jury. In an emphatic gesture, Earley pointedly and loudly ripped pictures from it as he described the losses Betty had suffered.

Finally, only two photos were left—a color picture of a stunning Elisabeth Broderick taken in 1975, and a black-and-white snapshot some ten years later of an overweight and disheveled woman.

"This is what was left," Earley said, gesturing dramatically to the more recent picture. "But I think that you'll see that it was someone who had no self-esteem. It was someone who had no way of dealing with problems. And I think that you'll see that she was acting on emotions that were thrust on her."

Some of those emotions became obvious to the jury when Betty sobbed as she listened to her lawyer recount the years of her courtship and marriage to Daniel Broderick. With the arrival of another woman, the marriage changed, and, Earley argued, so did Dan Broderick's attitude toward his wife. The defense attorney accused the dead man of trying to terrorize his wife psychologically:

"He started telling Elisabeth Broderick that she was crazy, [that] she needed to be counseled, that what she was seeing and what she was feeling was not really happening. Enough so that she started to doubt herself."

While carrying on a psychological campaign, Daniel Broderick was also maneuvering financially, Earley charged. He said that Broderick had moved money from joint accounts to investments controlled by his brother in Colorado in an attempt to reduce his community property liability after a divorce.

After the separation and divorce, Earley said that Broderick bombarded Betty with a "snowstorm" of legal documents, the equivalent of a "litigious assault." The fatal early morning visit was prompted by the arrival of yet another letter. She carried a gun because she was afraid of Dan Broderick and wanted to confront him without a threat of arrest, her defense attorney explained.

Further, he told the jury that evidence would show that Dan and Linda were awake when Betty fired, not asleep as the prosecution had contended. The gun went off when she panicked because someone yelled "Call the police!"

Kerry Wells had offered a much starker picture, of a woman whose "hatred for Daniel Broderick became the absolute focus of her life." Killing Dan and Linda Broderick was something Betty had been "talking about, thinking about, deliberating over for a long, long time," Wells maintained.

Her voice breaking with emotion, the prosecutor described how Betty had entered the house carrying the handgun, walked into the bedroom and fired at the sleeping couple, then ripped the phone from the wall while Dan "essentially was left to suffocate in his own blood and die."

Wells's clear vision of a premeditated, cold-blooded murder became a little murky when one of her first witnesses had to change his testimony on an important detail. San Diego police officer Terrence DeGelder said, on direct examination, that the ripped wires were tightly wrapped around the telephone lying at the top of the stairs. That implied that Betty had planned every move.

Presented with crime scene photos, DeGelder recanted, acknowledging under Earley's relentless cross-examination that the pictures clearly showed the wires trailing behind the dropped phone. Other graphic photos of the Broderick bedroom showed the bodies of Dan and Linda, twisted in bloodstained sheets. Betty did not look up as Wells displayed the pictures to the jury.

The prosecution played even stronger cards the next day, the first full day of testimony. Kerry Wells began with the straightforward scientific witnesses. Dr. Christopher Swalwell, the medical examiner, reported that Linda Broderick died instantly from the shot to the head, but the one that punctured Dan's lung took longer, probably a couple of minutes. A police firearms expert offered his professional opinion that the pattern of shots appeared to be a controlled aim, not "panic shooting."

After the dry technical witnesses, Kerry Wells offered more dramatic testimony—a series of thirty messages Betty had left and Dan had saved from the answering machines over eighteen months, from May 1986 to December 1988.

"I just want what's mine. That's all I've ever wanted. I don't give two shits about you. You're not worth spit," is the message in one. In another, she made a vague threat: "Fuckhead, you've turned my life into a nightmare. I can't go to sleep. I close my eyes and I see you and the cunt, and I see you doing all your wonderful things and, um, you're gonna be real sorry."

Wells also played the half-hour conversation with Danny, taped in 1987.

After the jury heard the dramatic, emotional call laced with Betty's obscenities, Kim Broderick was called as a witness against her mother. She remembered that her father had started the tape machine during that phone call because "Danny didn't usually get that upset." The rest of her testimony was equally devastating, especially when she repeated a conversation she had with Betty shortly before Dan Broderick married Linda Kolkena:

" 'I'm going to kill them. I'm going to shoot them.' She said she would shoot them in the head four times, three times," Kim remembered. Her sensational testimony was marked by tears, both her own and Betty's.

The young woman, only twenty years old, told of losing her key ring a couple of weeks before the shootings and how Betty helped her search for it. "My dad's key was a big deal," Kim said. "We were supposed to guard it with our lives." She also reported that her mother knew that Dan Broderick had recently taken out a two-million-dollar life insurance policy, one that provided a quarter of a million dollars to each of his children.

"She never said, 'Then we'd get the insurance policy,' " Kim testified. "But she said, 'We'd have money, we'd be rich.' She said that a lot."

In more than five hours spread over two days on the witness stand, Kim told other stories of life in the Broderick family both before and after the divorce. Betty often railed at her children to take her side against their father, Kim said, because she "just hated him and she wanted us to hate him." She said Betty had urged ten-year-old Rhett to run away from his father's house, and had even called him "a spineless wimp" for not standing up to Dan.

After the prosecutor read aloud an excerpt from Betty Broderick's diary, calling her ex-husband "the sickest person alive," Kim said that she had agreed to testify because "someone should tell the truth about Dad."

She also refuted some of the other accusations in the diary, that Dan Broderick had ever been violent toward Betty or that he had had a drinking problem. Kim admitted that her father "was not good with emotions . . . he had a hard time saying 'I love you.' When he was drunk, he could do that very well."

Cross-examined by Jack Earley, Kim conceded that Dan referred to Betty as "fat" and "crazy" and that she did not have a good relationship with her mother. "Mom and I didn't get along," she said. "I don't think she thought very much of me." Kim said that she and Lee and even the boys were often tagged with vulgar epithets when Betty was angry with them.

Once, she recalled, Betty didn't keep plans to see Kim's new apartment. When she called to learn what happened to her mother, Betty told the young woman that "all of a sudden, I remembered I hate your guts." Kim repeated the rest of that conversation with her mother: " 'You are a traitor. You make me sick. The sight of you makes me want to throw up. I wish you were never born.' "

If Kim's hostility was understandable, the next witness seemed to have no ulterior motive for her testimony. Linda David was a former housekeeper for Dan Broderick, beginning in 1987. She had met Betty often and considered her pleasant and charming, until the subject of her ex-husband arose.

"She referred to Dan in some very derogatory, profane terms, and Linda as well," David testified. "It was a lot of hatefulness about everything about him. She talked about killing him. I wouldn't say all the time, but it wasn't an uncommon thing to say."

When the housekeeper had tried to be encouraging, telling Betty she would find love again, "she kind of laughed and said that's not why she married Dan in the first place. She said she had married Dan because she knew he was going to be successful and a money-maker, and he had the same goals as her.

"She never talked about losing Dan's love or the relationship. She mostly talked about the loss of the money and status," David said. Another time, she remembered that Betty "made the comment that she was sure Dan and Linda would like her to disappear. She said that wasn't going to happen. She was going to make their lives a living hell or she was going to kill them."

The first week of the trial ended with testimony about Betty's life and her reactions that Sunday following the shooting of Dan and Linda. After a long legal argument over hearsay testimony, Patricia Monahan and Jerry Thatcher were allowed to recount the graphic and shocking phone call from Betty that November morning. Judge Whelan ruled that their testimony fell under an exception to the hearsay rule that allowed statements made spontaneously by people under stress, on the theory that they have had no time to think up a lie.

Monahan also had details of Betty's shopping habits, as did Helen Pickard.

"She loved money," Pickard testified. "She worshiped it. She was a very materialistic woman. She always was." Betty and Helen Pickard had first met fourteen years earlier, but Pickard broke off relations eleven months before the trial, after a troubling jailhouse call from Betty.

It came at the end of December, the day after Christmas and more than six weeks since the shootings. Betty said "her children would be better off with their father destroyed," Pickard recalled. She also remembered Betty saying that she blamed Linda Kolkena for "destroying my life, destroying my family, destroying my children, destroying my social life."

"I said, 'So you destroyed her?'" Pickard testified. "She said, 'Yes.'" She remembered that Betty "said it with a kind of laugh, like it didn't matter, like it really didn't bother her."

Even being in jail "didn't seem to have a major effect" on Betty, in Pickard's opinion. "I did not get the impression it was a traumatic experience," she said, adding that she didn't take any more calls from Betty after that. She characterized Betty Broderick as "obsessively jealous" and an "alcoholic spender" whose "closet wasn't big enough" for all the clothes she bought.

In the days just before the shootings, Pickard recalled that an "agitated" Betty was "really, really angry," afraid she would have to sell her house. On that Saturday morning, Helen remembered that Betty had said "Linda is leading my life" as they sipped coffee.

Betty sat stoically as the two women, both her former friends, made their appearances as witnesses against her. When her daughter Lee was called, she relaxed enough to smile slightly.

Lee's brief testimony as a prosecution witness focused on the Sunday morning nearly a year earlier when her mother had called to say

"I shot your dad. I shot the S.O.B." She said that Betty had talked about "pulling the phone out of the wall so he couldn't save himself."

"She felt empty and dead inside," Lee said. She remembered her mother's arrival at her apartment, Betty being sick, and then "I gave her a hug." Lee would have more to say as a witness for the defense.

Kerry Wells had one more day of testimony to present. She brought in Bradley Wright,-who did his best for Betty. He described her as depressed, even "suicidal," continually uncertain about when she could see her children. He recounted the problems she had had getting through to the boys when they were staying at Dan's house, and their complaints that they didn't have enough food at Cypress Avenue.

Wright also suggested that Betty's threats were not meant seriously, because she often said she would kill someone when she was angry or upset.

Sylvia Cavins, Dan's last housekeeper, also remembered hearing Betty make threats to kill her ex-husband: "I said, 'Oh great, he'd be dead and you'd either be dead or in prison and the children would be orphans.'"

The response, Cavins said, was "that would not be a problem because when a jury found out what Dan did to her, [they] would let her off. I said, 'I wouldn't count on that.'"

The housekeeper also remembered another threat, this one in the spring of 1989 around the time of the wedding. Cavins recalled Betty saying that she wanted to put "four bullets in Dan's head, one for each of the kids." Jack Earley pointed out to the witness that her police statement made six months after the alleged conversation said Betty planned to shoot Dan three times, not four.

"When did that get added to the story?" he asked pointedly. Cavins answered that "I must have meant four" when she first talked to the police the previous November.

One of the last of the prosecution witnesses was Kathleen Cuffaro, the associate attorney in Dan's office who had handled some of the divorce motions. She recalled problems with visitations, especially a weekend when Betty took Rhett to Lake Tahoe and then New York, although he was supposed to be back in Dan's custody.

Cuffaro said she had wanted Dan to appeal the final alimony decision and to prosecute Betty even more for contempt violations, but he disagreed. He was even talking about negotiating a new custody arrangement with his ex-wife because "he wanted to get on with his life," Cuffaro testified.

The final witness called by Kerry Wells was psychologist Ruth Roth, who had tried to mediate the Broderick custody dispute in the spring of 1987. She testified that the last thing Betty wanted was to let Dan "get on with his life." Roth referred to the notes she had made during three meetings in March of that year, telling the jury of Betty's promise that "I'm not going to be a single mother with four kids. He'll die first.

"I didn't think that she was psychotic, I think she was very angry," Roth said of the defendant. With that, Wells rested her case and turned the courtroom over to the defense.

12

WITNESS FOR THE
DEFENSE

A T LAST IT WAS BETTY'S TURN. ALL OF SAN DIEGO WAS GOING TO HEAR HER
story, told her way.

Although it is unusual for defendants to take the stand in criminal
cases, Betty's only hope of avoiding a conviction for first degree murder lay in her openness, her willingness to expose her pain to the jury
of her peers, the ultimate judges of her fate.

Having admitted firing the gun that caused the deaths of two people, she could not sit back, allowing her lawyer to work with the
presumption of innocence that is a fundamental of American justice.
Nor could she invoke her Fifth Amendment right not to testify against
herself. Her confession forfeited the advantage of making the prosecution prove guilt. She now had to prove herself not guilty of the
charge of first degree murder.

For years Betty Broderick had been pestering people to listen to
her complaints and pay attention to her view of what was happening.
The trial presented a unique opportunity to describe her emotions,
explain her actions, and blame Dan and Linda for the persecution she
had felt.

The book-lined courtroom was packed on the morning of Tuesday,

October 30, 1990, when Jack Earley called Elisabeth Anne Broderick as a witness in her own defense. The twenty or so seats for the public went quickly; anyone who left for any reason found their place usurped by one of the four dozen people still waiting to get in.

The family rows were also filled. Kim sat with Larry Broderick, who had flown in from Denver, and with two of Dan's sisters, from Pittsburgh and Seattle. One of Betty's brothers made the trip from Tennessee to be with Lee for what promised to be a difficult few days.

For those who couldn't squeeze into the crowded courtroom, the local TV stations had a pool camera taping the testimony. Channel 39 (KNSD) wanted to broadcast the testimony live as part of its "more aggressive" news coverage, but Judge Whelan declined permission for that.

For five hours an emotional Elisabeth Broderick talked about the early years of her marriage. She recounted her courtship and the hard times while Dan was still in school and she had two small children. When she recalled how she teased her husband by calling him "Dapper Dan," she began to sob. Whenever she referred to him or to his activities, she used the present tense, saying for example that Dan "loves clothes" or "looks good in clothes."

She remembered that he "apologized profusely" to her at the Marriage Encounter weekend in 1976 for not being "the kind of husband or father he wanted to be, or I should have . . . He said he wanted to be a very important man, a very prominent man, a very rich man. He needed to concentrate on those goals. We were almost there. If I would just give him more time, it really was for the children and me that he was doing all of it."

Betty said she accepted his explanation, trying to make the marriage work for the sake of their four children. She described her family as private individuals with a special need for each other: "We were each other's only intimates on earth."

Sobbing, she said, "Dan's opinion of me was really all I cared about. I didn't care what anybody else thought." She related the events of 1983, recalling how she felt when Dan called her "old, fat, ugly, boring, and stupid," and announced that he "just wasn't having any fun in life anymore." Her tears broke out again as she recounted her suicide attempt that year. After she burned his clothing and he told her he had spent the afternoon of his thirty-ninth birthday taking a deposition, "I felt like an idiot. I believed him."

When he left her alone with the children, she dropped them on his doorstep one by one because "I wanted Dan to get involved in our family." She called the sale of their home by court order a "totally unnecessary, brutal, ugly, bullying thing to do." Her response—ramming her car into his front door—was caused by frustration after Dan refused to talk to her in person: "I was upset. I'd never done anything like that in my life. I needed someone to listen to me."

The first day's testimony ended before Betty could get to the period of the shootings.

On Wednesday the lines were longer and the testimony even more agonizing. For the first few hours Betty continued her litany of complaints about the end of her marriage and the legal actions that ensued. Her voice rising and occasionally breaking, she described herself as the victim of a "left-right bam" in 1986 inflicted by Dan Broderick and his friends in the courts.

"Left to me was the kids' situation, with not being able to see the kids," she said. "The right was the sale of the house from out from under me with no control. And right between the eyes was cutting off all the money and being absolutely, totally unreasonable."

She talked about the barrage of legal papers and contempt citations through the years and her feelings on seeing another letter from the lawyers when she woke before dawn on Sunday, November 5, 1989. "I just couldn't stand it another minute," Betty recalled. "I'd rather be dead. I had no life left . . . I couldn't get out of the hole I was dug into by all this legal stuff."

Her birthday was approaching, she said, "and I was just standing in that kitchen saying, you know, 'Jesus Christ, I'm turning forty-two years old and I've been put through this shit since I was thirty-five . . . Seven years of my life wasted.' "

There were other things, too. Her "churning" thoughts recalled Dan and Linda "telling people I'm a child molester and I'm crazy and I'm an unfit mother." Or Dan telling her "it would never be over."

She left for the beach before dawn while "the kids were asleep.

Brad was asleep." On the way, she changed direction, going to Marston Hills to tell Dan Broderick that their long legal battle was "ruining me. It's ruining the kids. It's senseless." The gun was already in the car, and she took it with her as "a show of force, a way to make them listen."

Betty said she was afraid of Dan because he had abused her physically during their marriage—"bruised and marked up a little." She remembered a black eye, but said she "never got a broken bone." She wanted him to listen to her, but if he refused, she planned to use the gun on herself, "splash my brains all over his goddamned house."

While she drove to Cypress Avenue, she said, she was thinking, "I can't do this anymore. I can't go to court anymore. I can't go to jail anymore. I want to end it. I had to make it stop or I was going to kill myself."

Her voice flat, almost lifeless, Elisabeth Broderick recounted her year-old memories of the fatal moments on that early November morning: "I pushed the door open a little more than it was and I just stood in there and it looked like Linda moved and she went toward Dan, and Dan went toward the phone . . . I went in the room to talk to them or to wake them up or something, and they moved and I moved and it was over . . . I don't know what happened because it was dark. I didn't see. I didn't hear; everything happened that fast . . . I hardly remember being there at all."

She pounded the witness stand rapidly five times to demonstrate the shots she recalled hearing, but said she didn't remember pulling the trigger. Betty thought she might have heard Dan say "You've shot me" or possibly "Don't shoot," but she wasn't really sure. When she found no bullets left in the gun for herself, she "went to get out of the room, to flee . . . I grabbed the phone out of the wall and ran out. I didn't want him to call the police and have me arrested."

After her surrender, Betty Broderick said she slept soundly for the first time in years, "happy to be locked in a dark little safe room where no one could get me." Jack Earley asked if she was happy about what she had done, and she answered, "Of course not." Then she said that she accepted responsibility for the deaths of Dan Broderick and Linda Kolkena Broderick.

The distressing, emotional story could be seen throughout the county. Channel 39 broke into a soap opera for seven minutes of live testimony as Betty recounted those moments in the bedroom on Cypress Avenue. In the family seats the Broderick contingent wept openly. So did Lee and Betty's brother, sitting on the other side of the courtroom behind the defense table. At the end of the day, Kim and Lee embraced in the hallway. Betty, looking drained, hung her head in her hands and rubbed her eyes.

As difficult as the past two days had been, Betty Broderick still faced the challenge of cross-examination by Kerry Wells. That began on Thursday morning.

Under attack by the prosecutor, Betty conceded at times that she had forgotten some details of the long divorce battle, explaining she had been "under the most outrageous stress . . . I don't remember things, I don't remember being in court. I got legal papers. I honestly don't remember things."

Betty asked Wells for dates and details of the incidents she forgot, encouraging her with the words, "You keep trying . . . when you hit on something, then I can remember more." She explained that Dan Broderick "was telling me I was crazy. I went crazy." She panto-mimed herself as "an electrified crazy person," grimacing, sticking out her tongue and rolling her eyes in a demonstration of her feelings.

At other times during the questioning, Betty offered to correct Wells's remarks, once saying to the prosecutor, "No, you're all mixed up. You want me to help you?"

Wells tried to pin down the inconsistencies in Broderick's story, but frequently found the defendant wiggling out of her trap. Betty described the divorce proceedings as leaving her "bludgeoned" and "gang-raped" in "taped-up courtrooms." When the prosecutor pointed out that her attorney had also agreed to the closed hearings and sealed record, Betty replied, "It was never a big deal, it was just the principle of the thing . . . I would have stood on the highest building in the world to get help."

Discounting her obscene messages as "the only way I had to fight back," Betty admitted calling Linda Kolkena vulgar names, including "bimbo," "stupid," and "classless." She denied telling her sons to stab Linda, to gag on her food, or to call her names themselves.

While acknowledging several acts of vandalism, Betty also denied scratching a family photo, throwing an umbrella through a window, or harassing Dan and Linda at Kim's high school graduation by following them around with a camera. The story that Betty had threatened to kill the pair at their wedding was the "biggest of the black, horrid lies going around this town."

Wells tried to get details of the black eye, but Betty conceded she couldn't remember much about the incident, saying, "It was his elbow . . . It wasn't that big a deal." The prosecutor wondered if the incident wasn't the result of smudged mascara at a Bar Association dance, but Betty insisted she had been hit a few days earlier and used the mascara story to explain away the vestiges of bruising.

She said that she had earlier denied physical abuse in her marriage because "unless there were major, major injuries with broken bones and blood," she didn't consider the violence serious. Daniel Broderick's abuse was "somewhere in the middle. It's not an absolute."

The prosecutor pressed Betty on her complaints about finances, pointing out she spent $37,000 in 1986 on clothes. The defendant insisted she had no extra money and that Dan was ungenerous, offering her only $2000 to take the four kids skiing for a week over Christmas.

After the heavy emotions of the previous two days, Broderick remained calm throughout Wells's probing, often hostile, questions. Asked if she had been aware that she had to kill Linda as well as Dan to make sure there was no widow to inherit the estate, Betty responded coolly, "I hadn't exactly thought about it."

Like a boxer, Wells kept jabbing away at Broderick's story. She asked why Betty never got medical attention for her slashed wrists in the November 1983 suicide attempt. Betty said that "Dan was a doctor—he taped them," and the prosecutor wanted to see the scars. After looking at the wrists Betty held out, she announced that she didn't see any signs of cuts.

Jack Earley immediately objected, pointing out that Wells's comment was improper testimony. Judge Whelan agreed, striking the comment and allowing Betty to show her wrists to the jurors so they could decide for themselves.

As she moved in front of the jury box, her left arm extended, Betty said, "I did it with a man's razor with my right hand . . . that's one of the scars. That's one of the scars. That's one of the scars. I didn't die. Obviously it wasn't a good job, but I do have the scars."

The day of cross-examination was shown on Channel 39, which broke into regular programming, including "Geraldo!" and the soap "Generations," four times to offer live testimony. At 11:30 A.M. and 4 P.M., time slots the station considered "soft," the live broadcast went for most of the half hour and included expletives normally forbidden on television. News director Don Shafer explained that the station did not have the more complicated television facilities necessary for the seven-second delay used in radio call-in shows to prevent obscenities from airing. A crawl advised "viewer discretion," and Shafer reported most of the callers complained about the loss of the soap opera, not the language.

The complaints didn't keep Shafer from returning to the courtroom Friday morning for Betty's fourth day on the witness stand, her second under cross-examination. Wells continued to bombard her with pointed questions designed to play up her inconsistent comments and memories. When the prosecutor accused her of trying to avoid answering, Betty said, "I'm not lying. I'm trying to help you, and help me, get it right."

Denying any personal feelings toward Dan or Linda, Betty explained she was angry at what they had done: "I did not like what Linda Kolkena did to me or my family. I hated what Dan Broderick was doing to me and my children . . . In my estimation, Dan and Linda never suffered for a minute through the seven years me and my children suffered tremendously."

They disagreed over the seriousness of Betty's threats to kill Dan and Linda. "I probably said I was going to kill him a million times before," Betty said of her use of what she called a "catch phrase." It was an exaggeration, like the comment she had made to a recent visitor saying, "I love it in lock down in Las Colinas jail. It's the happiest I've ever been." But "obviously, it's not the happiest I've ever been," she said.

Her most emotional response came after a question about her handwritten note, "I can't take this anymore," scribbled on the letter that had arrived on Friday, November 3, from Dan Broderick. It threatened more contempt of court citations if she continued to leave obscene messages. After the long years of the divorce fight, Betty Broderick said the letter meant that Dan was "still attacking me, bludgeoning me, taking unnecessary advantage of me."

Her voice rising dramatically, Betty Broderick denied any premeditation, describing her thoughts on that Sunday morning almost a year earlier: "What did Dan and Linda have to gain from not letting me speak to my sons? And just fucking me over? I couldn't stand it another minute and I had no plan. I died when I wrote that stuff. I wanted to die and I had no plan. I just wanted to just, just, die. That's it. That's the end of the story."

Betty rejected Wells's accusation that her story had changed, saying, "I have never changed my story, because there's only one story." She again recounted her actions on that November morning. She had the gun with her, she said, because "I was deathly afraid of Dan Broderick. I was afraid of him attacking me and maligning me and threatening me to take the children and to lose the house and I'd never see another red cent from him."

She insisted that her memory was spotty; she could recall entering the house and walking up the stairs, but after that, "I know I went to Dan Broderick's house and shot a gun in the dark . . . I didn't know whether I hit anybody, I didn't know what to do, where to go."

That gave Wells another opening. If Betty was so confused and upset for so many years, how did she show so much organization and control after her arrest? The prosecutor pointed out that Broderick had quickly changed magazine subscription addresses, wrote out instructions on paying bills and caring for her condo for Brad Wright and her daughter Lee.

"Someone had to take care of those things," Betty answered.

Wells also tried to show that Betty had exaggerated Dan's ambitions, getting her to acknowledge that she had not objected to his decision to start his own law practice even if it meant a few more years of limited earnings. When the cross-examination ended, Jack Earley introduced into evidence Dan Broderick's booklet from the Marriage Encounter weekend in 1976.

The jurors could read his comments for themselves: "I tell myself that I've got to earn a decent living, establish myself as a lawyer, acquire certain necessary possessions before I can indulge the luxury of being an attentive, thoughtful person."

After the day's testimony ended and Betty was excused as a witness, Larry Broderick expressed his feelings about his former sister-in-law to reporters outside the courtroom: "I believe this woman is an incredible monster. Dan had to put up with her greed, avariciousness, and hate for his entire married life and five years after that."

Apparently unconcerned that Kim was standing nearby, the forest products executive from the suburbs of Denver said he "was outraged at what this woman did to my brother for twenty years."

Kim described her own feelings toward her mother as "confused," saying, "I don't want her to suffer, but, at the same time, she should be punished for what she's done."

It took Jack Earley another week to present the rest of the defense case, trying to limit Betty's sentence to something less than life in prison. He called in a succession of witnesses to bolster his arguments that Dan Broderick had purposefully acted to drive his ex-wife over the edge; that the actions during and after the marriage constituted abuse, both physical and emotional; that Betty was driven beyond her limits when she entered the bedroom on Cypress Avenue that November morning; that she had gone there to talk, not shoot, and that she had left Dan's house so shaken, she was unaware that anyone had been hurt.

On the first anniversary of the deaths of Dan and Linda, Jack Earley called an Arizona psychologist who specialized in postshooting trauma. Stephen Carson said he served as a consultant with a dozen police departments. He testified that research had shown that reactions to stress followed a well-charted path that often caused police to forget the exact details of a shooting incident.

Under cross-examination, Carson acknowledged that his studies were on people who had been suddenly confronted with a shootout. He had no data on those who had planned a shooting deliberately and carried it out.

Don David Lusterman, a clinical therapist from Long Island, was called as an expert witness on the effects of extramarital affairs. Talking generally from his research findings and not specifically about the Brodericks, the psychologist discussed the "uncapped volcano of pain" that develops when an unfaithful husband lies to his wife.

The woman, Lusterman said, goes from "cold rage" to "hot rage" and may eventually burst into "a sudden and explosive reality." The wife, feeling "utterly, totally betrayed," may be suicidal or threaten her husband.

Betty Broderick wiped away tears as she heard Lusterman describe how such wives must "look toward the perpetrator of that pain for the resolution of that pain." The expert witness talked about the "tremendous sense of unreality about her very being" for the woman who has been deceived, a pattern he said was common in his experience over seventeen years of practice.

"She wonders how she could have been such a fool," Lusterman said. "[She] tends to blame everyone," because she has a "very, very deep wound . . . Everything she has been told has been called into question . . . every day has been filled with lies."

Even Betty's harrowing conversations with her sons and daughters followed the pattern the psychologist expected in such a situation— "ineffectual as a parent . . . [and] unthinkingly cruel to their children." The "victim" uses the children for her own ends, to send messages between the feuding parties or to validate her own view of the situation.

"The children get put in the line of fire, like Saddam Hussein taking his hostages and putting them in the line of fire at strategic points," Lusterman said, providing a colorful metaphor a few months before hostilities against Iraq broke out.

On cross-examination by Kerry Wells, Lusterman acknowledged that he had not spoken to Betty Broderick, but had offered his opinion based on his clinical research and an outline of the case from defense attorney Jack Earley. His years of experience with hundreds of angry couples had not included a murder case before, "only tremendous physical outbursts."

Wells asked him if factors such as a "narcissistic personality disorder" in the abandoned wife and an "ex-husband who attempted to settle honorably" made a difference in his analysis. Lusterman did not respond specifically, explaining instead that any healing process had to include an admission of responsibility from the unfaithful partner and an "honorable" settlement.

The next defense witnesses offered support for Lusterman's analysis. Three of Betty's friends testified about the change in her appearance and attitude after Dan Broderick walked out. They also recalled that she blamed everyone around her for her divorce.

Longtime friend Marilyn Olson recalled that Betty felt "she was a victim of the legal system." As a result, Olson said "there was a long and ongoing series of changes . . . a basic loss of control and depressions and acting out and panic."

Melanie Cohrs also noticed the difference: "I saw that she ate a lot . . . gained a lot of weight . . . didn't seem to care as much about her appearance."

Anne Dick had known Betty for thirteen years. She called her friend the "consummate mother," saying that she often left her young son with Betty because "I couldn't have left him with anyone better." Dick had also put a young husband through law school, and defended Betty's attitude about money, explaining that after so many years of hardship, "there's a certain amount of gain one is preoccupied with."

All three of the women recalled a Betty Broderick more often dressed in sweatsuits and tennis shoes than the designer outfits and evening gowns the prosecution had emphasized. None of the three could remember Betty swearing uncontrollably in their presence, but Melanie Cohrs related how frustrated Betty would get if she could not get through to her children when she called them in Marston Hills.

Tuesday produced a string of nearly twenty defense witnesses, ranging from two of the judges who had presided over parts of the Broderick divorce to the grocery clerk who sold Betty the half coffee, half cocoa, she took on her early morning walks at the beach.

155

The judges agreed that the Broderick divorce file disappeared before the trial late in 1988, then reappeared. They said the missing parts of the file were not important to their decisions. Neither had any idea of where it had been. Their testimony was brief.

Several more of Betty's friends were called to the witness stand. Evangeline Burt and Phyllis Jardel both remembered seeing her with a black eye, but Jardel also recalled that "she didn't really accuse Dan" of giving it to her.

Other friends testified to the changes in her personality since 1985. Judith Backhaus said Betty was "outrageously funny" before the troubles with Dan began, and Candace Westbrook noticed "drastic changes," Betty was no longer "up, happy, positive." Bible study leader Candace McCarty first knew Betty in 1984 and said she was a "mother that beamed around her children." But longtime maid Maria Montes said her employer was "always sad. The only time she was happy was when the children were present."

Speaking through a Spanish interpreter, Montes recalled that the boys didn't like living on Cypress Avenue and "several times hid in the bushes in the backyard so they wouldn't have to go to the father." When the boys weren't staying with her, Betty "was always crying."

Bradley Wright was recalled to testify for the defense. He described a woman who was often "upset and depressed." In the four years that he had known her, Wright said, Betty "liked to be alone by herself, not with the family and friends."

A plastic surgeon from La Jolla offered testimony that bolstered Betty's story of an attempted suicide in 1983. Dr. Ross Rudolph said that he had found two small scars on her left wrist, adding they were not "particularly deep."

Jason Prantil, Lee's boyfriend, also supported a part of Betty's story. He recalled her appearance and conversation on that morning one year and one day earlier. He said that she "was talking very fast and she wasn't making a lot of sense.

"She was very incoherent," Prantil recalled. "Among her ramblings, she said she wanted to confront him about resolving the situation." That matched Betty's testimony that she went to the house in

Marston Hills planning only to talk to Dan and Linda, not to shoot them. Firing was a panic reaction, not a deliberate plot.

After Jason, Jack Earley called Lee back to the stand, this time as a defense witness. Now he was not limited to the topics raised by the prosecutor in direct questioning, but could explore his own areas.

The first was Dan's temper. Lee talked about the names her father had called Betty, the way he reacted to frustration by breaking things. She recalled that he kicked the family dogs. Betty would warn the kids to stay out of his way when he was upset, Lee said.

Dan was angry with her, too, Lee testified. After she dropped out of school, he "disowned me." She said that he had told Kim he would change that "once things were straightened out" after she finished an equivalency program and received her high school diploma. Because Lee lived with Betty at Calle del Cielo part of the time, she wasn't allowed to have a key to her father's house. If she arrived at Cypress Avenue unexpectedly, "I'd knock on the door, and if nobody was home, I'd have to go somewhere else."

As for Betty, Dan didn't want to see her or speak to her, Lee said. He didn't use vulgarities when he referred to her; "crazy, sick, and disgusting" were among his terms of choice, according to Lee. She recalled how Dan and Linda would instruct her younger brothers to pressure Betty, telling them to ask her "if she was crazy, and if she was, why didn't she go to the doctor? If she did go to see a doctor, they'd be able to see her more often."

Lee's testimony also raised some questions about one part of Betty's story. Lee remembered when Kim lost her keys. "My sister and my mom looked for the keys together," she said, but she never heard that a set of keys had been found.

Betty had testified the key ring had turned up in her house and she wasn't sure where it came from. When no one claimed it, she put the strange keys in a box of miscellaneous junk being moved to her condo. That's how it ended up in her car, and her hand, when she went to Dan's house that Sunday morning.

Lee's testimony seemed to contradict her mother. If Betty had helped Kim search for the keys when they were first lost, surely she would have remembered who they belonged to. Further, Betty said

157

she thought her maid had found them, but Maria Montes didn't remember hearing about or finding lost keys.

The defense lost another battle that day as well. Jack Earley hoped to have one more witness testify. Wilma Engel had talked about Betty Broderick's troubles with Dan to another lawyer, and it got back to the medical malpractice specialist. Earley wanted the jury to know about the letter Engel had received from Dan. It threatened to tell her husband that she had an affair if she continued to talk about the Broderick divorce. Judge Whelan ruled the story irrelevant to the trial.

On Wednesday the defense offered more testimony to show Betty's changing moods. Lucy Peredun had lived with Betty rent-free during the last half of 1988 in exchange for light housekeeping. She remembered a woman who was "pleasant" and "nice." Peredun said "the use of bad language was not frequent—seldom if ever," and when her sons were present, "Betty was just a bubble of energy."

Dian Black talked about the strange early morning phone call she got from Betty after the shootings. "The way she told me was, 'I shot at them. It was dark,' " Black recalled, adding that she could hear Betty sobbing and vomiting. When they met later that day, she thought Betty, who had been "very depressed" for several months, "was in shock." Black said that she had "never seen Betty that way in her life . . . It was like her body was there but it was a shell."

Jack Earley had one more important witness, but he would not be available for another day. To save some time, Wells began presenting her rebuttal case. Brian Forbes remembered riding in Betty's Jaguar late in 1985 and hearing her threaten to kill Dan. "She made light of it," Brian Forbes said, but he considered it "serious enough that I was concerned about it and brought it to Dan's attention." Forbes also remembered Betty telling him then that she had a gun, "just a little one." He recalled the weapon as a .357-caliber Magnum, although the gun used on Dan and Linda was a .38-caliber revolver bought in March 1989.

The final defense witness was Dr. Daniel Sonkin, an expert on domestic violence. He told the jury that Betty Broderick had been a victim of physical abuse and sexual battering as well as emotional abuse of "the most destructive . . . signifying a betrayal of trust." A licensed marriage counselor in Sausalito, Sonkin said Betty had told him that Dan Broderick "came home intoxicated on numerous occasions and forced her to have sex."

On information provided by several interviews with Betty and members of her family, friends and Lee, Sonkin cited examples of Daniel Broderick's behavior that were abusive: "He choked her, he grabbed her, he pushed her down . . . he called her names . . . a yuck, crazy and stupid. He degraded her as a woman. It happened even while they were dating."

Betty Broderick was a definitive battered woman in Sonkin's expert opinion, a victim of "a cycle of violence." When she had "her identity ripped away" by Dan Broderick's affair with Linda Kolkena, she was "overwhelmed," according to Sonkin.

It was his professional judgment that Betty was "physically, sexually, and psychologically abused, that the separation and divorce was devastating to her, and that a lot of her behaviors that we saw or that were written about or talked about . . . during the time of the divorce were the result of this devastation that she was experiencing psychologically."

For Kerry Wells, it must have been infuriating. The battered women she was used to defending had bruises and broken bones, swollen eyes and fat lips, not swollen egos and fat bank accounts. She began her cross-examination by attacking Sonkin's credentials.

He held a doctorate in marriage and family counseling, but was not a medical doctor nor a licensed clinical psychologist. His experience in domestic violence came, in part, from consultation work for the military and law enforcement authorities. Wells didn't seem impressed, and the psychologist appeared uneasy by her lack of respect. As her questions became more pointed, Sonkin's previous erect and friendly posture slumped. He snapped his responses, often interrupting the question.

Sonkin had interviewed Betty, her family members, and her friends, but had not spoken to any members of Dan's family. He admitted that Dan and Betty had spent more time with his family than with her relatives during their marriage. Under Wells's probing, he explained it was not customary for expert witnesses to interview all available sides, but emphasized that several people had told him about seeing Betty with black eyes and bruises.

Wells asked for specific dates, but Sonkin was unable to provide any. The prosecutor probed further. The witness insisted that Betty's erratic actions were symptoms of domestic violence, "signs of how overwhelmed she could be at times." Wells, her voice showing her emotions, asked why Betty had never mentioned abuse until she was charged with murder. Sonkin replied that "if she is minimizing, you know it's probably worse," but acknowledged there were inconsistencies in Betty's story.

The prosecutor produced the statement of Gerald Nelson, a psychologist who had been a witness during the dispute over custody and alimony and found Betty "perfectly rational." Wells read from the transcript of Nelson's testimony at the January 1989 hearing:

> "If she murdered Mr. Broderick, as she has threatened to do, she could never be called incompetent. This lady knows what she is doing; she is very bright, very determined to get her share of the assets and to get her way."

Then Kerry Wells produced a report written three years earlier than Nelson's, when Betty was under observation after ramming the door on Cypress Avenue in February 1986:

> Intolerance of inactivity and an inability to delay gratification are associated with her impulsiveness, shortsighted hedonism, and her minimal regard for the consequences of her behavior, which may lead to difficulties with legal authorities.

The report added that Betty's "energies may be devoted to clever deceptions designed to seduce others into supporting her immature or irresponsible excesses."

Sonkin said that those were among the "voluminous" reports he had read on Betty Broderick. They didn't change his opinion that her husband's behavior pushed her "deeper and deeper" into "craziness." He had considered some of the conclusions of the other experts—that she was a "borderline personality" with "histrionic," "narcissistic," "manipulative," "violent," and "suicidal" traits—but Sonkin insisted those characteristics were not inconsistent with a battered woman. Betty, he said, was too embarrassed to admit it: "I think the most telling thing was, when I interviewed her, she said, 'I'm not a battered woman.'"

Wells asked about the incidents of vandalism and obscenity-laced telephone messages, suggesting that they made Daniel Broderick a victim of abuse, too. Sonkin rejected that, saying, "No, I don't believe Dan Broderick was a victim." He said although Betty may have been verbally abusive to Dan in public, the response was a private retaliation.

"I don't believe that marriage is a one-way street, that Mrs. Broderick is this victim and Mr. Broderick is this terrible monster who abused her," Sonkin hedged.

The psychologist answered a few more questions Friday morning, admitting that Betty was given to exaggeration, but saying she had "a lot of anger, a lot of hostility, a lot of hurt" from Dan Broderick's actions. Sonkin agreed that "it was inappropriate" for Betty, as a victim of his abuse, to continue to seek out Dan for help, but said that the medical malpractice attorney had "used the courts," not physical violence, to control his ex-wife.

Once Sonkin was dismissed, Kerry Wells worked to restore Daniel Broderick's image in her rebuttal case. She called the housekeepers who remembered how he played basketball and tried to have dinner with the children regularly. Marta Shaver flew back from Ohio because she felt "morally obligated." Betty had talked about Dan's drinking bouts, and Shaver disagreed. For the sake of the children, she wanted the story straight: "I never saw him have more than one or two glasses of wine in a month."

Robin Tu'ua had the story of Betty's threats in 1986 and 1987. The day she brought Rhett back from school and told the governess she had a gun in the glove compartment, Tu'ua said, "there was not a shadow of a doubt that this woman would use it on me."

Brian Forbes's wife, Gail, was also a rebuttal witness. She remembered the phone call from Betty at the women's jail on the evening of November 1, 1986. "Her tone was excited" as she asked Gail to notify the society pages of her arrest on the evening of Dan's triumph, because "this would be an event."

There was a bright spot in Betty's day. Three weeks into the trial, her father came from New York after all. He walked into the courtroom for the first time Friday afternoon, sparking a pleased grin from his daughter when she spotted him.

Frank Bisceglia should not have been surprised to find Betty's trial was the talk of San Diego, as it had been for more than a year. Over the weekend, the *Los Angeles Times* reported that everyone had watched her testimony and almost everyone had an opinion. "I don't think there's been one trial that has generated this much public interest in San Diego in the last ten years," said Don Shafer, the news director at KNSD, the station that broadcast the trial.

He suggested the universal fascination with the case was due to "a high BQ—bizarre quotient." Shafer reported that the early complaints about a preempted soap opera were quickly replaced by viewers who wanted to know when to set their VCRs to tape Betty's testimony.

The article reported that the trial was the topic of conversation from beauty parlors in La Jolla to fighter pilot ready rooms at the nearby Miramar Naval Air Station. Most people seemed to agree with a cosmetologist who offered her perspective: "I don't have any doubt that I think her husband, Dan Broderick, was a total jerk. But I still don't think he deserved to die."

Local experts on human behavior and social trends said the interest in the case developed because it had so many layers that touched familiar chords for so many people. "Other women may identify with Betty," explained one. Another thought the trial touched "on what we don't like to think is our own possibility in life, if we became so angry and driven, that we might kill . . . We don't think we'd kill another person. But we might."

The general public was even more confused. A cashier at a soup restaurant thought the trial was "like watching a soap opera, a soap opera brought to real life." The receptionist at a quintessentially San Diegan combination of tanning salon, gym, and Laundromat, thought that Betty was "pretty crazy." She and her friends believed "she wasn't justified in what she did . . . there's no reason to kill anybody."

By then most of San Diego also had access to exact details of Broderick family finances from a column by Paul Krueger in the *Reader*. By checking records at probate court, he found some evidence that Betty's claims that Dan had been manipulating their joint finances had a basis in reality. Krueger had uncovered several aspects of Daniel Broderick's tangled business practices that raised questions, as well as some strange decisions by the estate lawyers.

Dan's estate totaled just over $1.25 million. That included ten Canadian maple leaf coins, a 1974 MG Roadster, and a 1989 Sun Ray Sundance yacht—(eventually returned to the finance company that made the purchase loan)—as well as several evidently poorly chosen business investments. A Colorado bank wanted nearly a half-million dollars back on a loan for a Denver office building that had foreclosed at a loss. There were a few smaller claims stemming from other failed business plans.

Several other civil suits prompted doubts about Dan's legal and personal decisions as well. A local anesthesiologist had filed a $6.3 million malpractice claim against Daniel Broderick for allegedly mishandling a discrimination suit against a hospital that had denied her staff privileges. The trustee of Dan's retirement fund reported evidence of mismanagement to the court, specifically an unsecured loan of nearly a half-million dollars to Larry Broderick, who had never repaid a penny and was now executor of Dan's estate.

One of his responsibilities was the monthly checks to Dan's children. The four younger Brodericks had each received more than $80,000 in insurance money, and were still awaiting payment from their share of a two-million-dollar policy from Manhattan National Life and a smaller one from Hartford Life. All but Lee, who had been written out of his will, were also getting regular checks from the estate's bank account.

Dan's former sister-in-law, Larry's ex-wife Kathy, was getting more than $4500 a month from that account to pay for the boys' living expenses in Colorado, including rent and their share of utilities. In addition, the estate was paying another $20,000 a year for their private school tuition and vacations. Kim's monthly check was nearly $3500 to cover her living expenses as a college student in Arizona. The total included $275 for phone calls and $500 for car expenses.

Linda Kolkena's family decided not to challenge the ruling that she died first, so her estate reverted to Dan. Still unsettled a year after her death were claims from six creditors, including the El Camino Mortuary for a funeral bill of $7000.

The lawyers from Dan's former law firm, Gray, Cary, Ames & Frye, now representing his estate, filed two claims against Betty. In the first, they demanded that she return more than $13,000 of the $16,000 alimony payment she received for November 1989. The court papers argued that because Dan died on the fifth, Betty was entitled to only that proportion of the total.

The second claim, a wrongful death suit, was okayed by a probate judge. Usually the heirs file that kind of suit, but Kim and Lee declined to sue their mother. Linda Kolkena's family also rejected the option, saying they "wanted to put this behind us." The lawyers had no hesitation, however, about bringing a suit on behalf of the boys, who were still minors. The judge okayed the use of money from their share of the estate to pay the legal fees.

There were still more civil suits on the horizon. Betty's lawyers wanted to get the attorneys from Gray, Cary removed, or at least prohibited from representing Larry Broderick as guardian of Danny and Rhett. Her brother Frank hoped to be appointed their guardian, but that decision was put off for a year. The civil suits promised to go much longer than the criminal case, which was finally nearing its conclusion.

The trial judge was facing some important rulings first, however.

In a final bit of legal business before the trial ended, Judge Whelan rejected Kerry Wells's argument to limit the jury's choices to a conviction for murder or acquittal. The district attorney's office maintained that the manslaughter choices under California law, voluntary and involuntary, did not apply to this case. Voluntary requires sudden provocation to lead to a killing, and involuntary is used in cases where death results from an action performed without due caution. Betty Broderick's actions did not fit the statutory definition.

Judge Whelan decided to give the jury all five options anyway: murder in the first degree, demanding a finding of premeditation; second degree, if the defendant had lacked deliberation; the two manslaughter choices; or not guilty. The trial was almost over.

The final prosecution witness, Dr. Melvin Goldzband, gave as his professional opinion that no increase in alimony, custody arrangement, or property settlement would have satisfied Betty Broderick. "She wanted Dan. She wanted not to be rejected," said the medical school lecturer and author. Goldzband, who specialized in forensic psychiatry, said that Betty's problem—mixed personality disorders— was characterized by histrionic and narcissistic behavior that reinforced her need to be perfect and the center of attention.

As an example, he cited his interview with Betty Broderick when "she told me how perfect she was, as a mother, as a wife, as a person." When that image is questioned, he said, "the usual response is rage, they usually act out against the people who would dare to besmirch the perfect image."

Goldzband, who also had a private practice, said he had interviewed Betty within a week of his testimony and found her "severely narcissistic." That led to her feeling "grossly rejected" and "gloriously victimized" by Dan's decision to leave. "It's a characteristic of the necessity to dramatize her plight," the psychiatrist explained. "This woman has invested in her own sense of martyrdom, and this is what she has been demonstrating all this time."

Betty's pattern of calling friends to tell them of her latest acts of vandalism fit his diagnosis, Goldzband said, because "her behavior, in her mind, is always justified, reasonable and explainable . . . The point to be made is that her attitude toward her behavior is such that it is constantly justifiable . . . The idea that it may have effects on other people is totally alien."

The expert witness did find some special qualities in the Broderick case: "This lady ran roughshod over her kids much more than I've ever seen . . . The kids very transparently became a tool that she used to get back at her husband. Nothing else was as important to her . . ."

But Goldzband found some positive traits, as well: "This lady is charming . . . This is one of the most engaging of these people [criminals] that I've ever seen." He also added that she was intelligent, having read one of his books.

Jack Earley's final witness agreed that Betty Broderick had histrionic and narcissistic traits, but psychologist Katherine DiFrancesca did not consider them as serious as Goldzband did. She said that Betty's most serious problem was a borderline personality—a poorly defined sense of identity which brought on a state of "stable instability." In one interview, Betty had even told the clinical psychologist that she felt like "a dinghy boat on the ocean."

The psychologist said she had spent twelve years working for the county court system doing evaluations, and explained why she disagreed with the prosecution witness: "Some think they are really great. Some wish they were really great. Mrs. Broderick . . . wished she was really great."

DiFrancesca, who specialized in forensic questions for the San Diego County mental health division, added that Betty also suffered from serious depression. The end of her marriage, and the loss of her core identity as Dan Broderick's wife and the mother of his children, brought about a "total breakdown as the years progressed and the stress progressed."

She felt "devalued," DiFrancesca said. Women in Betty's situation "are rageful. They are devaluing everything around them." Even the obscene messages were a symptom. They are "so explosive," she said, the language "really shows how out of control she was." The stress she was under, DiFrancesca explained, caused Betty to lose the "executive function to control emotions." She tried to hide her feelings by being "energetic" and "a little madcap." Her acts of vandalism, all of her actions, were not thought out or planned, but done "spontaneously."

Kerry Wells rejected that position totally in her closing argument the next day. Betty Broderick's actions, the prosecutor maintained, were the result of a "smoldering, constant hate" that led her to "ambush" Dan and Linda.

"You do not point a .38-caliber gun loaded with hollow-point bullets at two people lying in a bed only inches away, early in the morning, and fire without intending to kill them," Wells said.

In the packed courtroom, Wells emotionally pleaded the case for a verdict of first degree murder against the defendant: "The law does not allow a person to charge into other people's homes with a loaded gun, to confront them, catch them totally off guard, unprotected, helpless, and kill them both and then say, 'But gosh, I didn't really mean it. I shouldn't be reponsible.' She's responsible for murder, period."

Jack Earley took the opposite position. His client had pulled the trigger that resulted in two deaths, he conceded, but "her act was one of craziness, one of emotion, one that should never have happened." It did, he said, because Elisabeth Anne Broderick was "out of control," unable to stop herself any more than a "boat without a rudder."

Kerry Wells didn't accept that argument for a moment. Suicide was not an option for Betty, the prosecutor said, because "if she did that, clearly Dan and Linda would have won." The tapes of Betty's obscene phone messages, especially the conversation with Danny, were the "essence of the entire case," Wells insisted, showing her "selfish and cruel."

Ticking off the various people who had heard Betty's threats to kill Dan, the inconsistencies in her story, and the awful results of that early morning visit, Wells described Betty Broderick as the "most incredible uncredible person you will ever come across in your life . . . She's awfully selectively forgetful."

Jack Earley, too, allowed his voice to rise dramatically in his last chance to defend his client. During his long argument, which continued after a lunch break, Earley discounted the obscene messages, saying "I don't even think that in the case of 2 Live Crew [tried in Florida for obscene record lyrics] there was more time spent on those issues than in this court."

He agreed that Betty had made some bad decisions and that there was "no good excuse" for the conversation with Danny, but Earley said the jury should not "make a moral judgment and based on that moral judgment say she should be convicted of a crime."

Why not question instead "a man who hears that distress but says, 'My job as a lawyer, making cases, overrides any other concern I have,'" and turns on the tape recorder instead of comforting his son, Earley asked. He talked about Dan's other legal tactics, and he compared his client to Martha Mitchell, the Cassandra of the Nixon administration.

The wife of former Attorney General John Mitchell made late-night phone calls to reporters about Watergate before she was exiled to New York and died suddenly. Both women, Earley implied, had tried to tell the world about influence-peddling and conflict-of-interest shenanigans among the powerful and protected, and both had been ridiculed and attacked publicly by the men who felt threatened by their revelations.

"There was no premeditation and deliberation in this case," the defense attorney insisted. "This was not the act of someone who wants to be the princess and the victim."

The closing arguments took most of the day. On Thursday, November 15, one year and ten days after Dan and Linda were killed, the jury began deliberating Betty Broderick's fate. First they listened to Judge Whelan instruct them on points of the law, including an admonishment that self-defense was not an option.

Betty showed her own disdain for the label she had received from prosecution psychiatrist Goldzband. She arrived in court that morning dressed in navy sweatpants, tennis shoes, and a gray sweatshirt stenciled S.D. JAIL rather than the more fashionable ensembles she had been wearing throughout the trial. Before the jury entered, she was seen mouthing the word "narcissistic," a reference to the doctor's testimony. She even sent a note to Judge Whelan saying, "I refuse to dress out." Later in the day she whispered that she was "protesting."

Defense attorney Jack Earley said she was still upset because the judge would not allow all ten volumes of her diaries into evidence. Betty had also wanted the jury to get more of the details from her divorce file and property settlement, but the judge ruled against her on that, too.

For the next four days the twelve people in the jury room wrestled with the evidence, the testimony, and what it all meant. They emerged Tuesday afternoon, one day before what would have been Daniel Broderick's forty-sixth birthday, to announce that they were deadlocked.

Judge Whelan declared a mistrial.

13

The Year of Living Dangerously

THEY WERE GOING TO HAVE TO DO IT ALL AGAIN.
The first reaction from almost everyone was frustration. The newspapers hounded the members of the jury to learn what went on in the deliberations. The jurors just could not agree. Ten had believed Betty was guilty of second degree murder, but two had insisted they could not accept anything higher than voluntary manslaughter.

"Malice was the sticking point," Charles Henderson, one of the ten voting for murder, told the *San Diego Tribune.* "That seemed to be what the majority of the discussion centered around. That and pre-meditation."

The auto mechanics instructor at San Diego City College also said, "I personally felt she was provoked. I think she was provoked for almost seven years. I felt like she was a victim. Now I'm not saying that she was justified, but I think she was pushed and that she ultimately was victimized, too."

Another juror spoke to the *Los Angeles Times* and described heated discussions "with three or four people believing that buying a gun constitutes a murder conviction." The anonymous panel member also blamed the deadlock on "several people . . . in a hurry to get home for Thanksgiving and not have their plans disrupted."

One of the two jurors who held out for manslaughter explained, "It was done in the heat of passion." He believed killing "was out of character" for Betty, but that the latest letter from Dan was "the straw that broke the camel's back." Juror Walter Polk, a retired Air Force engineer, told an interviewer for *Mirabella* magazine that his only question after hearing the evidence was, "What took her so long?"

The inconclusive result added to the Kolkena family's pain. Linda's sister, Maggie Kolkena Seats, had returned to her home in Portland, Oregon, just before the mistrial was announced. She had made a special trip to San Diego to defend her sister because "she's kind of been the invisible person through all of this."

Seats said Linda was not "an illiterate bimbo," as Elisabeth Broderick suggested, but a "bright, funny" woman who had insisted on paying her own bills even after her marriage. Determined to show her independence, Linda borrowed money from a finance company so her family could attend her wedding. Seats, a personnel officer for a utility company, said her family tried not to think about the outcome of the trial because "no punishment can bring her back." But she expressed the hope that Elisabeth Broderick would be "in prison for a long, long time."

Linda's father, Arnold, was contacted by the *San Diego Tribune* at his home outside Salt Lake City and admitted his disappointment: "I've always had faith in the judicial system. I wish they would serve justice. Maybe that will happen. What other way is there?" The older man said attending the trial of his youngest daughter's killer "would have been too hard on us."

Kolkena said Linda's family had decided at her funeral not to be bitter and unforgiving. "We said that's one thing [Betty Broderick] is not going to accomplish," he explained. "She's not going to poison our mind with hatred and affect us for the rest of our lives. It's a terrible thing she did. It would only destroy us. It wouldn't accomplish anything."

Betty's own children were also having a hard time. Kim Broderick, who had attended the trial daily, spoke for her younger siblings shortly before the testimony ended. The experience had been very strange, she said, watching strangers fight over which of her parents was "the bigger jerk." She came to the defense of both her mother and father: "They were great parents, but at different times. Obviously, my brothers and sister and I love our parents and didn't think either was a jerk."

Kim also wondered about the accuracy of the picture that had been presented in the courtroom of the Brodericks of La Jolla. "If I didn't know better, I'd think what a stupid, materialistic, superficial family . . . That's not how my family was."

And the final outcome left her as confused as ever. "There's no good answer," she said. "None. If Mom got out tomorrow, I'd feel like Dad was gypped. On the other hand, if they were to tell me she was going to prison for life, I don't think that's fair, either. I don't think she's a danger to society. I just think she needs help."

Betty's close friend, Dian Black, described her feelings on hearing of the mistrial as being close to shell shock: "I feel like I've been shot out of a cannon. I was looking forward to taking a vacation and curling up in a fetal position. It's like, here we go again."

Both lawyers were also frustrated by the jury's inability to reach a decision, although Jack Earley must have felt some gratification to know that his defense had been successful enough to prevent a conviction. Betty was reported by jail authorities to be in bubbling spirits at the inconclusive result, but her lawyer later said that "she had no idea if it [the mistrial] was good or bad or indifferent . . . I don't think you could say she's relieved."

Pleased or not, Betty Broderick had no choice. The state of California and the county of San Diego planned to put her on trial for murder again. Everyone was back in Whelan's courtroom one week after the mistrial to begin discussions for the next round.

That post-trial hearing was very brief. It took only a few minutes for Betty's lawyer to make his points. The first was a request for a bail hearing. The second announced that Elisabeth Broderick was indigent and could not afford whatever bail was set, nor his fees for the second trial. The bill for the first trial was almost a half million dollars and had left Betty broke.

After the hearing, Earley talked about a third point he planned to raise; the next trial should not include the charge of first degree murder. His investigators had spoken to all the jurors and they had agreed Betty was not guilty of that. Some thought there had been a vote, while others were only sure of their own feelings about first degree. It was Earley's position that a second trial on first degree murder charges was double jeopardy.

The prospect of bail upset Dan's brother Larry. After the jury's deadlock, he pointed out that his former sister-in-law "has never, since the whole sordid ordeal began five or six years ago, attached any import to the law. Second, she has threatened to murder me. I'm inclined to take those threats more seriously than I would have a year and a half ago."

The December 6 bail hearing was postponed for a week, but Larry Broderick, who had flown in specially from Denver to make his case to Judge Whelan, was allowed to speak at the shortened session to save him another trip. He called Betty Broderick "an evil monster in a harmless-looking package" and predicted "bloodshed" if she was given bail.

"If this woman is released on bail, if she shows up in Colorado, I fear, we fear, and the court should probably assume, that there will be bloodshed," he argued. As the former guardian of Betty's two sons, he informed the court that the boys were still "fragile, but they're progressing." Broderick said the boys' therapists had warned that any contact with their mother "would be a disaster for them." He accused Betty of threatening to kill her sons, a charge Jack Earley rejected completely, labeling it as "grandstanding."

In any event, a week later Whelan refused to grant bail: "I have to consider the protection of the public. I'm aware of the comments made . . . by the brother of Daniel Broderick. I'm aware that the defendant is accused of having committed two violent crimes and that she's admitted to having killed two people. I'm aware that, at one time, the defendant freely carried a firearm and that she still faces the

possibility of life in prison without parole. Thus, I find that a continu-
ance of her no-bail status is fully justified."

Whelan also ruled that the charge of first degree murder could
remain. Earley threatened to appeal that decision, saying, "The jury
was not properly instructed on whether they should vote to find her
guilty or not guilty of first degree murder. Because they were never
instructed to take such a vote, they never reached a decision on
whether she was guilty or innocent of murder in the first degree."

By the end of the year most of the decisions on the second trial had
been reached. Betty had filed as an indigent, and Jack Earley had
been appointed to defend her at a cost to the county's taxpayers of at
least $60 dollars an hour. He planned to ask for $180 to $200 an hour,
down from his usual fee of $250 for an hour's work. A trial date of
August was also set, but that, too, was dependent on Earley's maneuvering other cases on his schedule. In fact, it would take most of the
year before the second trial began.

The defense lawyer had other clients to consider. Between Betty's
two trials, "I tried a federal fraud trial which was taking a million
dollars from a federal savings and loan, that was about a four-week
trial; I tried two other murder cases and two other trials," Earley said.
"Plus my house burned down. So it was a busy year, a fairly substan-
tial busy year."

Jack Earley's recital left out a couple of details, like his surgery for
cancer on his lip. And the fire at his house in Laguna Beach, sparked
by a short in a VCR, caused damages estimated at $300,000, forced
his family to move four times over the next few months, and burned
up transcripts, phone lists, and witness summaries necessary for the
second round in court. That pushed Betty's trial date into September.

And, although the principal players were the same, more preparation had to be done for the second trial. The prosecutor was obviously
going to question the jurors about the weak spots in her case and
strengthen them. The defense, too, had to be ready to find counter-
arguments and new ways to undermine the prosecution's presentation.

"At the first trial we basically put everything on, so it's kind of hard
to change your tactics in a second trial," Earley commented. "We did

change our tactics with theirs. The first trial, if they didn't address the crime scene, I wasn't going to address it. In the second trial, I knew they were, so we got witnesses ready and faced that head on to begin with. So that was something that was decided. That changed the strategy somewhat."

Sitting in his relatively small office in a high rise in Newport Beach, the windows looking toward the mountains in the distance, Jack Earley responded to the accusation from parts of the San Diego legal community that he had put Dan Broderick on trial instead of the real criminal: "These cases are never about trying the victim. The victim is part of the facts. If you're a mean, nasty person, then people are going to respond to you that way. If you're a nice person, people are going to respond to you that way.

"All those civil lawyers, that's what they do for a living," Earley pointed out. "That's what negligence is, it's proving what the victims do. So what you end up having . . . they were all part of the facts. How can you understand Betty's actions in a vacuum?"

The defense lawyer's comments seemed slightly contemptuous of his colleagues who specialized in negligence. It was a surprising area of agreement with courtroom foe Kerry Wells, who also had no interest in that branch of the law.

"My dad was a civil lawyer," she explained. "He always wanted me to come work for him and stuff, and I never had any interest in doing civil law. Fighting over money is not to me where it's at. I wanted to go into criminal law from the very beginning."

Her office, too, was in a high rise, but in downtown San Diego with the windows looking out on the bay. The Coronado Bridge arced across the sky, giving a twenty-first-century look to the view. A photo of Dan Broderick and Linda Kolkena topped one file cabinet. Snapshots of the prosecutor's own children sat on another one. On her door hung a poster showing a casket with a vase of flowers and the caption: "He beat her 150 times, she only got flowers once."

Wells found the prospect of a second Broderick trial unappealing, but she was determined to finish what she started. "Hung juries, to begin with, are real frustrating," she explained. "I always kind of feel like that's the worst that can happen . . . because on a not guilty, as

long as twelve jurors listen to the case and they get both sides . . .
and that's the determination they make, then that's the way the system works. A hung jury, it just feels so like the entire system
failed. . . .

"This hung jury was really, really frustrating," she went on. "We'd
put a lot of work into it, a lot of effort. I worked full-time on the case
for a year, and then to think about having to try it again . . . It was
not a pleasant experience going through this trial . . . I was very
disappointed that I would have to try it again."

The case continued to attract attention even during the hiatus. The
Ladies' Home Journal article came out in March 1991. So did a *Los
Angeles Times* interview with Betty in jail. She seemed pleased to be
there: "It's been wonderful. Just what I needed. I'm very slowly but
steadily turning into a human being that functions again."

She talked about the possibility of a plea bargain and denied that
the shootings had been motivated by jealousy and revenge.

"That was the kind of thing that everybody wanted to believe it was
at the beginning," she said. "But that had nothing to do with it.
Leaving me for a younger woman. That had nothing to do with what
happened subsequently.

"[I've] never been jealous of Linda Kolkena for a moment in my
life," Betty insisted. "Ever. I'm not jealous of her. Never was. In fact,
I looked down my nose at her."

Had she been out for revenge, Betty told her interviewer, things
would have been different: "I'd tie them up where they couldn't
move and I'd torture them every single day and single night for six
years. I'd leave them at night where no one could hear them screaming, come back and give them cigarette burns and kick them, like
torturers do. Because that's what it felt like they were doing to me."

In comparison with that time, jail was "a vacation." She received
hundreds of letters a month from sympathetic people, mostly women.
Some of her correspondents had even bought her magazine subscrip-
tions, so she had lots of reading material. So much, in fact, she was
punished by being sent to a solitary cell. Even that didn't bother her.

"I love it in lockdown," she explained. "It's bigger, it's quieter. I
can exercise. They hate that. They're trying to make you unhappy."

The period after her separation and divorce had been like "having alarms and bells and sirens going off in your head nonstop for years. It really wears you down. Then I had depression besides. It felt like, 'Emergency, emergency, bells, bells, lights, lights, save yourself, save yourself.' I was trying to save myself every way I could think of, but nothing was happening."

The past fifteen months behind bars had been relaxing, allowing her to rest without any pressures. She told the newspaper reporter that prison was like "a country club. A tennis court, a swimming pool, you walk around, no stress, no responsibility. I wouldn't have to worry about getting my car fixed. I can read. I can converse with people. I can write."

But she did have one complaint about it: "It's early retirement. But what a waste. I'm too young to waste like that."

The plea bargain offer was made the next month, in April. Betty missed her children and hoped by pleading guilty and receiving a fixed sentence she could start planning on her release. She offered to plead guilty to a mixed variety of charges—assault, kidnapping, and burglary—for a sentence of twenty years, making her eligible for parole in about fourteen.

San Diego County district attorney Edwin Miller rejected the offer. Kerry Wells explained that "unless she's willing to plead guilty to murder, other charges . . . are all trumped-up charges. That's not seeking justice. If she's guilty of something, she ought to be guilty of what she did. Let's not put charges together to put years together. That's not the way we work."

Earley agreed to change the plea to manslaughter, but that wasn't enough, either. Denying that he was under pressure from Dan Broderick's friends to get a murder conviction, Miller insisted, "I think it's a murder case . . . All I can say is it's our intention to take the matter to trial. It's our view that the case should be tried."

Most prosecutors like plea bargains. They save taxpayers the cost of a trial, they save prosecutors court time, and they assure that a person guilty of a crime will spend time in prison. It was certainly not unusual for any district attorney to agree to a guilty plea of manslaughter for a murder case. Most homicides involving women killed by possessive men are bargained down.

Given Miller's assurance that he was not getting any pressure from the powerful legal friends of the victim, his insistence on trying Betty Broderick for murder still raises some questions. If there was no pressure, what was the purpose of trying her for first degree murder? Could it be to send a message to other women?

Apparently, the men were already far beyond the reach of any message, so plea bargains were okay for them. The FBI statistics for 1989, the year Dan and Linda died, show that ninety percent of the more than 2600 female murder victims in the United States were killed by men, more than a fourth of those by husbands or boyfriends. By contrast, only five percent of the more than 7800 male murder victims had been done in by their wives or girlfriends.

It is hard to escape the feeling that someone in San Diego wanted to see Betty Broderick convicted of first degree murder, no matter what it took. Jack Earley would later say it took a decision to limit the evidence she was allowed to present.

"I think what happened is that they said give the woman her day in court," the defense attorney said. "Let her say whatever she wants and let her bring in what they want, and she's going to get convicted and there'll be no appeal. What happened was, she wasn't convicted the first trial, so they knew that they couldn't let everything in. They had to keep a lot of stuff out if they wanted to get a conviction."

One of the first indications of how different the second trial was going to be came in June. Five months earlier Kerry Wells had asked Judge Whelan for permission to see the confidential psychiatric files of doctors who had interviewed Betty for the defense but did not testify. Whelan had ruled that turning those over to the district attorney would violate the constitutional right against self-incrimination. The D.A.'s office filed an appeal. In a precedent-setting opinion, California's Fourth District Court of Appeal overturned Whelan's ruling and Wells got the files she wanted.

Another difference was a cocounsel for Kerry Wells. For the second trial, Paul Burakoff, a fraud specialist, would be sitting at the prosecution table, too. They had worked together before, and Wells insisted that Burakoff was "my choice," not foisted on her by supervisors being pressured to produce a guilty verdict against Elisabeth Broderick.

Betty had one bright spot at the end of that summer. She got her dearest wish. She was allowed to see her sons again. It was her first personal contact with them since she had left them peacefully sleeping in Calle del Cielo that Sunday morning almost two years earlier.

For the past year, she had been forbidden to speak or even write to them. Twice in that time judges had rejected her pleas to send them cards on their birthdays or holidays. Their visit to her at Las Colinas was short, only an hour, and heavily restricted. She still wasn't permitted to say anything to them about the case or her feelings about her situation or even their living arrangements with Dan's former sister-in-law, now divorced from Larry.

The second trial was scheduled to begin at the end of September, but the month began with more bad publicity for Betty. Like all such situations, there was either a strange series of coincidences, difficulties, and circumstances converging, or it could have been kicked off on purpose.

According to Jack Earley, the incident began on August 22, when Betty was chained to another prisoner whom she considered to be violent. When she screamed for attention, she was charged with breaking the rules and given four days in isolation. The jail officials said Betty impatiently grabbed for the deputy's hand holding a set of keys, and that's what the punishment was for.

When the guards arrived to take her to isolation the following week, Betty Broderick fought them. Wearing only a gray jail-issue sweatshirt and green underpants, she held on to the railing of the top bunk, kicking and struggling while the deputies tried to pry her loose. One guard stood back from the fracas, putting the whole thing on videotape.

Jack Earley found some unusual coincidences: "It was interesting that the district attorney's office . . . served a subpoena [at the jail] asking for any videotapes made of Elisabeth Broderick. Then, lo and behold, a week later, a videotape is made."

The tape turned up on local television stations about a month after the melee, and just two days before jury selection was scheduled to begin for the second trial. According to both Wells and Earley, one of the deputies injured in the battle with Betty stole it out of the sheriff's locked safe and turned it over to her attorney, who handed it out to the media. Although the sheriff's office did investigate how the video got out of the locked safe and turned up on the local news, no sanctions were pursued against those responsible.

The strange incident provided more charges and accusations. Wells claimed that Betty, angered at being put in isolation, smeared excrement over the cell's walls and windows. Jack Earley countered by saying the cell's toilet was broken and overflowing, and Betty, upset and hurt, "ended up going to the bathroom in her pants. There was nowhere else to go."

Three deputies were reportedly injured in the fight; one hitting her head on a bracket when she fell backward after Betty allegedly kicked her in the chest; a second had scrapes and scratches, and the third hurt a shoulder. Wells said the scuffle could mean more criminal charges against Broderick.

The incident first came to light shortly after it occurred when Wells asked for a gag order in the case, hoping to prevent Betty's scheduled interview with ABC's "20/20" news magazine program. Whelan denied the prosecutor's request, and Betty was released from the isolation unit briefly to do the interview with reporter Tom Jarriel.

Betty, apparently unstoppable even behind bars, contacted local journalists when she was out of isolation. She told a male reporter for the *Los Angeles Times* that the whole isolation thing was exaggerated, commenting, "They sure are getting their mileage out of their tape." She said she was embarrassed by the "pistachio-green" underpants and the way she looked, then added defensively, "If you were locked up in a teeny-tiny little room for two years, you'd have flabby thighs, too."

ABC was not the only national news medium interested in the case. A long feature article about the upcoming trial appeared in the *New York Times*. Another one showed up in *Mirabella* magazine's September issue. The Broderick case, with all of its complexities, hit the headlines again at a time when the problems between men and women generally were the "hot" topic.

In the months since Betty's first trial, there had been some unexpected developments in the way the two sexes perceived and related to each other in the United States. There was an ongoing national debate about credibility and gender and discrimination and provocation between the sexes. A series of incidents had combined to produce a national consciousness-raising of sorts. A lot of old assumptions were being questioned, and a few new insights were brought forward.

It had begun in the spring, when William Kennedy Smith, the nephew of Senator Edward Kennedy, was accused of raping a thirty-one-year-old woman over Easter weekend on the beach outside the family compound in Palm Beach. A few weeks later former heavyweight boxing champion Mike Tyson was also accused of sexually attacking a beauty contestant who had accompanied him to his Indianapolis hotel room on an early morning date. Many men said both accusers were asking for sex by their actions; women generally believed the charges and challenged the arrogance of the opposite sex's assumption of right.

Then came the Senate hearings on the appointment of Clarence Thomas to the Supreme Court. The lineup of white, male senators taking pot shots at law professor Anita Hill and ridiculing her accusations of sexual harassment against Thomas infuriated women throughout the country. The senators' female colleagues from the House, led by Colorado congresswoman Pat Schroeder, marched across the Capitol to proclaim their outrage: "They just don't get it."

While Wells and Earley were still choosing the jury for the second trial, National Public Radio broadcast a "Horizons" program called "The Case Against Women: Sexism in the Courts." It reported that nineteen states had been studying the courts after protests from women, and all had found evidence of rampant discrimination. Women's complaints were taken less seriously, women's testimony was considered less credible, and women defendants faced longer sentences for violent crimes.

There was another change at this second trial. In the twelve months since the mistrial had been declared, Court TV had come into being. The cable channel, the creation of Steven Brill, publisher of more than two dozen local and national legal newspapers, presented unedited courtroom testimony. About half of the country's households wired for cable could get the new channel, and the Court TV producers had already decided they would be present for Betty's second trial.

This time Betty would have a national audience for her story.

14

The Verdict

O N TUESDAY, OCTOBER 15, 1991, THE RETRIAL IN THE CASE OF
California v. *Broderick* began. It was exactly fifty-one weeks
since the opening arguments of the first trial. Some similarities were
strikingly apparent. Judge Thomas Whelan still had thick gray hair
and still sat back in his leather armchair, but now he had a full year's
experience as a judge. Jack Earley again sat next to Betty Broderick at
the defense table. She had gained weight and her hair was a brassier
blond than before. Across the aisle Kerry Wells looked appropriately
professional, dignified and confident. But the prosecutor's table was
different. Next to Wells sat her cocounsel, Paul Burakoff, another
deputy district attorney.

And the jury was different. That was the whole purpose of doing it
again.

How different had apparently been foreseen by Dan Broderick's
brother, Larry, in the months between trials. He had discussed the
weaknesses of the prosecution in the first trial with many of Dan's
legal colleagues, and they had developed tactics to shore them up. In
a letter mailed to the district attorney in June, he outlined the sugges-

tions. They came to light when a copy of the letter was sent to the *Los Angeles Times* anonymously during the trial.

Perhaps the most controversial tactic was the proposal that witnesses "take the opportunity to ramble on a little about Dan and Linda" until the defense was forced to object. The evidence thus introduced, even if "hearsay and inadmissible," would have an impact on jurors that were "of lower-middle class, less than average intelligence."

Broderick explained in the letter that "while the words are mine, they represent the consensus view of the group." The newspaper story identified the group as including two current officers of the San Diego County Bar Association, Brian Forbes—who was a prosecution witness—and several of the lawyers representing Larry Broderick, or Dan Broderick's estate.

When contacted, the attorneys denied having any part in writing or sending the letter, but most admitted discussing the case. Jack Earley contended the letter was proof of Betty's charges that "the deck was stacked against her." He also said that "eleven of the twelve suggestions mentioned in the letter have already been followed." The only exception was Larry Broderick's proposal that the testimony of his adolescent nephews, fifteen-year-old Danny and twelve-year-old Rhett, be timed "to have the greatest possible lasting impact on the jury."

That jury had been chosen after three weeks of voir dire, including another lengthy questionnaire. The prosecutor's table had expanded further to accommodate a consultant who helped Wells and Burakoff with their decisions. The five women and seven men were younger than the first jury. The oldest this time was a fifty-nine-year-old widow; the youngest, two twenty-year-old women students. One man was a convicted burglar, another admitted he had thought about killing his ex-wife.

Several jurors were current or former Naval Center employees or otherwise connected with the defense industry. Unlike the first panel, which had included an executive and a couple of mid-level managerial types, this one consisted mostly of blue-collar workers, electricians, technicians, machinists. The foreman was a medical librarian.

When the jury filed in for the opening arguments, there were some obvious and subtle differences from the scene a year earlier. One news story commented on the "amazing resemblance" between Linda Kolkena and a young Betty Bisceglia. That seemed to signal a reduced level of hostility toward the defendant. Local fascination with the case appeared to have waned. There were empty seats in the small courtroom.

National attention was just beginning, however. Court TV had picked up thousands of viewers with its coverage of the Senate Judiciary Committee hearings on the Clarence Thomas nomination to the United States Supreme Court. The Broderick trial was its next full-time case. Halfway through Betty's trial, the cable channel began showing jury selection for the rape trial of William Kennedy Smith in West Palm Beach. That resulted in an even larger audience. East Coast viewers could watch jury selection from Florida in the morning and the Broderick trial live for the rest of the day.

The opening arguments were very similar to the first time, but there were some signs of new tactics. Props got more attention. Jurors and national viewers took a videotaped tour of Dan Broderick's home on Cypress Avenue, following the route Betty took that November morning.

Jack Earley also added some drama. Brandishing a framed photo of the Broderick family, he smashed it over the lectern: "Glass didn't protect a family. It was shattered, and Elisabeth Broderick tried to hold the picture together."

Earley repeated his accusation that Dan Broderick was trying to terrorize Betty, describing her as "gaslighted, from an old Charles Boyer movie, when you want someone to appear different than they really are. He was showing that she was crazy and that justified his behavior. Dan Broderick controlled what the marriage was about and he told her, 'You have no right to be angry.' His reputation was so important to him that he had to destroy Betty Broderick so she would not talk and would not be believed about the private Dan Broderick."

Kerry Wells, of course, had a different view: "It was not an impulsive rash act. She made deliberate choices every step of the way. She had the gun in her hand, ready to use. She knew the layout. She went through the Broderick home in violation of a restraining order, just another one of the rules she didn't have to obey."

Brian Forbes was an early witness this time, graphically describing "like cookies and cream ice cream," the bloody froth near Dan Broderick's body. The prosecution also offered its technical witnesses, including the medical examiner and one of the first police officers to arrive at the house. Jack Earley picked away at the minor changes in their testimony: Forbes didn't remember wanting to call an ambulance; DeGelder avoided the trap, saying he didn't recall the cord being wrapped around the phone.

The most significant change was in the testimony of Dr. Christopher Swalwell. The pathologist had altered his opinion and now believed that the bullet that struck Dan Broderick in the back had only broken the skin of his chest wall. It was not a "through and through" wound. Swalwell said the wounded man probably could have survived if he had had medical attention.

"The example I usually give is President Reagan," the deputy medical examiner said. Under fierce cross-examination from Earley, Swalwell was asked again if the wound was "through and through." He backed off a bit, saying it "could have been."

In a graphic illustration, desexed foam dummies were punctured with dowels to show the path of the bullets. Like ghosts, the dummies stood propped against a wall once they had served their purpose, a visual reminder of the crimes charged.

After the first day of trial the defense attorney accused the prosecution of getting subtle changes in the testimony: "I think the district attorney needs a certain scenario in the case, and I expect that their witnesses are going to supply that." Wells disputed the charge, saying, "We're not trying to change any theory."

For the second day, Wells played the long, painful tape of the conversation between Betty and her son Danny. The jury tried to hide their feelings as they listened. The defendant cried openly. Kim testified about the recording of that call and other details of life in the Broderick households. Reporters noticed she seemed less angry at her mother, even explaining in court that: "I love her, but I'm mad at her. I don't like the things that she's done."

Kim recalled asking her mother why she had killed Dan and Linda, and said the answer she received was: "My choice was to kill them or myself. I couldn't let him win." But when queried about going into her mother's purse, Kim glanced at Betty and smiled before responding: "I don't know if she always wanted us to go into her purse, but we did." When her testimony continued the following week, Kim again smiled at her mother as she took the witness stand.

Betty's attorney was less friendly. As Jack Earley hammered away at discrepancies in her testimony, Kim Broderick finally lost the calm she had maintained throughout the second trial. "Yes, I remember testifying at the first trial, Mr. Earley," she snapped at one point, "but a lot of things have happened to me since then." When Earley persisted, the young woman put her head in her hands and sobbed briefly.

The defense attorney continued his attack, asking if she had "talked to anyone earlier about giving long answers." Trying to show Kim's hostility toward her mother, Earley also probed her feelings for Betty. A fresh-faced young woman with a slight vagueness, Kim regained her poise quickly.

"Mom and I got along fine some of the time and fought some of the time," she answered. "If I had known when I fought with Mom that this was going to happen, I would have been nice to Mom every minute of every day."

After the trial Jack Earley accused the prosecution of abandoning the oldest Broderick daughter. "Kim was left out in the hallway with nobody talking to her," the attorney said. "All during the trial, the D.A. and all Dan's friends would come up to her every day and grab her and kiss her and tell her what a wonderful girl she was and walk her out of the building." Once the trial ended, Earley said he saw Kim sitting alone on a bench in the hallway, unnoticed by the prosecutors or her family.

As before, Kerry Wells called a string of former housekeepers and governesses to the stand. Robin Tu'ua and Linda David recalled confrontations and conversations with Betty that included threats to Dan. Gail Forbes remembered Betty's glee at nearly forcing Dan off the road. Forbes also recalled Betty bragging about her skill with a gun.

When Ruth Roth took the stand, Jack Earley was better prepared. During his cross-examination he forced her to admit that the interview with Dan Broderick was the only time in her career the psychologist did not take notes. Roth also acknowledged that she later treated Danny in private therapy paid for by his father, and had sued Betty for an uncollected fee for the mediation attempt.

One new prosecution witness was a former cellmate of Betty's. Maria Peralta first met Betty Broderick in December 1989, shortly after her arrest. The self-described "working girl" said that Betty "never showed she was sorry or anything." A former heroin addict in jail on prostitution and drug charges at the time, Peralta added that Betty had said that Linda "has been in my bed for seven years." The jail informant also recalled her cellmate commenting on her marksmanship, saying, "I guess I'm not as good as I used to be. I had five and I only got three in."

Admitting that she had refused to testify for the prosecution last year, Peralta said that she had changed her mind over the summer and contacted Kerry Wells. Her request to be paid for her testimony was a joke, she said, explaining that "being a working girl, we never do something for nothing." The *San Diego Tribune* reported that Peralta had tried to sell her story during the first trial, refusing to give the interview when her demand was rejected.

Kerry Wells then called witnesses to back up Peralta's claims. Patricia Monahan and Jerry Thatcher recalled that early morning phone call from Betty with its horrifying details. Lee made her brief appearance for the prosecution again. Lee seemed to be a more complicated personality than her older sister. Her face is thinner, her eyes more deeply set than Kim's. Lee's haunted look made her appear slightly older, more knowing.

Housekeeper Sylvia Cavins again remembered Betty threatening to kill Dan Broderick, saying, "[Betty] was not happy with their happiness. She detested them, she hated them both." Cavins also recalled hearing Betty talk about taking target-shooting lessons.

There was more testimony about Betty Broderick's marksmanship. New witness Stephen Frantz remembered running into her at a local indoor pistol range and noticing her skill. The attorney said he remembered the incident because the woman had told him she was Dan Broderick's wife.

A San Diego Police Department ballistics expert offered his opinion that the shots were "well-directed, well-placed, accurate shooting." Eugene J. Wolberg said it was "bordering on the impossible" that the wounds were accidental. The firearms instructor also explained that the barrel of the .38 revolver was too short, so the hollow-point bullets didn't explode as they were supposed to.

The jury passed the small handgun around, then Kerry Wells rested her case. In eight days of testimony over a two-week period, she had called more than two dozen witnesses. There were no major changes from the testimony presented in the first trial. The big differences would come during cross-examination of the defense case.

Jack Earley began slowly. His first witness was a resident of Marston Hills who remembered hearing five gunshots "one after another" about 5:30 A.M. on Sunday, November 5, 1989. After William McCauley's appearance, the trial was recessed for two days, giving the defense team time to round up its witnesses.

When they reconvened on Halloween, a plastic pumpkin graced Kerry Wells's briefcase, the court reporter sported pumpkin earrings, and Jack Earley spread bloodstained sheets over the double bed in front of the jury box. Only the sheets weren't holiday decorations. Betty was seen crying at the defense table when the bed was set up. She stopped before the jury entered the courtroom.

The defense attorney called two forensic experts to prove that Dan Broderick and Linda Kolkena were awake and moving when they were shot. Taking advantage of the opportunity, Wells and Burakoff brought back the foam dummies pierced with dowels. When the jury returned from a recess, the prosecutor picked up the handgun entered into evidence and dramatically demonstrated her version of events on that Sunday morning nearly two years earlier.

Earley later acknowledged that the bloody sheets had been "risky. It's always risky to do that . . . I hope the jury understood that you can't come in and say, 'There was a person lying here, and a person lying here, and they were asleep or not asleep . . . The whole thing about the bed was just to show that there is no way of telling what was going on in there, that there was obviously a lot of movement."

There were more surprises. Betty's longtime maid testified about the day Linda Kolkena had come to the house on Calle del Cielo and removed "some documents" from the master bedroom. They were returned "four to five hours later." It happened early in 1989, just after Betty had taken the list of wedding guests from Dan's home.

Maria Montes remembered that Kolkena was in the house when she arrived. With the help of an interpreter, Montes explained that when she "heard noises, I said, 'Hello, is anybody in the house?' And she said, 'It's me. I'm a friend of Betty's. I came to see the house.'" Jack Earley explained later that Linda was at the house while Betty was in court, responding to a four-hour notice threatening a contempt citation if she didn't return the invitation list.

The final surprise came at the end of that day's testimony. Jack Earley had called Brian Forbes back as a defense witness. He hoped to impeach his previous testimony with the letter from Larry Broderick. Waving the five pages, Earley angrily asked Forbes if he was part of a plan "to get things out in front of a less-than-middle-class jury?" Forbes admitted that he had seen the letter, but denied being part of a conspiracy. Wells objected and the exchange was stricken from the record.

The next day, Judge Whelan tried to straighten things out further. Before testimony began, he told the jurors that the comment about a "less-than-middle-class jury" had not been made by either of the attorneys in the case and did not reflect their opinions in any way.

Betty's father was the next defense witness, describing the phone call he got from his daughter that Sunday morning. Frank Bisceglia had been in court for the first full day of defense testimony, too. This time Betty's mother had come with her husband to San Diego, but Marita Bisceglia sat outside the courtroom reading a prayer book. She told reporters she had a cold and "didn't want to worry Betty Anne."

Betty did have her own concerns. She took the stand after her father and again related the story of her courtship and the early years of her marriage. Jack Earley tried to introduce the two booklets from the Marriage Encounter Weekend in 1976 as he had during the first trial, but Judge Whelan upheld the prosecution's objection. Kerry Wells had argued that Daniel Broderick's comments were "prejudicial." The defense attorney said outside of court that the prosecutor specifically meant Broderick's remarks about the Catholic Church. Earley expressed the hope he would be able to get the journals in later during the trial.

On Monday, Betty resumed her narration of the events and emotions that brought her to that darkened room on a Sunday morning nearly two years earlier. She described as "gang rape" one court hearing during the divorce when Superior Court judge Anthony Joseph greeted Dan warmly. Then, Betty said, the judge had turned to her and "explained that he was a longtime friend of Dan's and that he held him in very high regard. He asked me if I would have a problem with that. I said, 'Do I have a choice?' And he said, 'No.'"

She elaborated on Dan Broderick's physical abuse, accusing him of breaking her sternum with a punch, giving her a black eye, and when she accidentally crossed his skis, "he hit me so hard, I went flying through the snow. I hurt my ankle so bad, I couldn't walk." Betty detailed her search for an attorney who was equal to her husband's skill. She explained away the changes she made in the divorce papers filed with the court because "I'm a schoolteacher and I circled things and wrote in the margins. I corrected it."

It was another day before she talked about the morning she drove to Marston Hills. In an eerie coincidence, Elisabeth Anne Broderick described those moments in that darkened bedroom on Cypress Avenue exactly two years to the day after the shots rang out. Her dramatic emotional testimony was seen across the country.

She began sobbing when she again recalled her emotions as she stood in her kitchen before dawn that morning twenty-four months earlier and looked at the letter from her lawyer. "This meant I was not going to get the kids for the whole school year probably," she said through her tears. "I was going to have to waste money fighting in court about stupid things, and Dan was just going to jerk me around and mess up the money undoubtedly with the fines . . . and if he fined me like he used to fine me and take money away . . . all those moves I was making to take control of my life and make decisions were totally dependent on that monthly check, and if he pulled the monthly check everything would come crashing down."

Under Jack Earley's careful questioning, Betty recounted her thoughts and emotions on that November morning. "I felt so victimized," she said, her voice rising dramatically. "And then I was angry . . . This is all happening at once in my brain. I'm explaining it one thing at a time, but it's all at once . . . What are they doing? Why are they doing this to me now? Why can't they just leave me alone to get control of my life and get my kids and have a peaceful, normal life?

"I didn't know what kind of sick jollies they were getting out of driving me crazy! And I'm saying to myself, what do they want out of me? What the hell do I have that they want now? And the only answer I could come up with is that they wanted to drive me crazy . . . It was sadistic, what they were doing. There was nothing else that I could give these people to get away from them. So I just went out of the house. I was going to go down to the beach."

But on the way there, she changed her mind. Betty explained how she decided on one final confrontation with her ex-husband. She wanted "to ask him for the kids and just leave me alone . . . If he wouldn't agree at all, I was just going to kill myself in his house, not down at the beach, not at my house." The gun was in her purse in the car, and she brought it along "initially in order to make them have to talk to me. If they said they were calling the police, I'd say, 'No you're not!' If he wouldn't deal with me, give me the kids, I was just going to kill myself."

Jack Earley asked her "how were you seeing the world" on that morning as she drove to the Broderick house.

"The only way to describe it, I had all these thoughts churning in my head," Betty responded. She raised her hands, one clutching a white handkerchief, and they circled and flailed in front of her face as she put her emotions into words. "There was so much going on inside my head, like my eyeballs were turned backwards. The whole world was inside my head because of all this anguish, so I wasn't seeing where I was going. It was like I was just inward . . . All this anguish . . . darkness . . . crazy thoughts."

Once again Betty Broderick described her disjointed memories of the confrontation in the bedroom: "The motion I made, although I don't think it was a big motion, the movement I made into their bedroom woke them up and they moved and somebody screamed, 'Call the police,' and I said 'No!' and I just fired the gun and this big noise went off and then I grabbed the phone and got the hell out of there, but I wasn't in that room . . . it just was an explosion . . . I moved, they moved, the gun went off it was like *aaahhh*!!! . . . it was that fast."

Aware that Kerry Wells was going to ask more questions about those few seconds in the bedroom, Earley tried to lessen the effect by going over the specifics himself. There were more details compared to the previous year's brief "they moved, I moved, it was over" description. Betty explained her memories were "like a slide show" but "slides are missing." She couldn't recall saying anything, and insisted her visual memories were of dim shapes and vaguely moving figures.

"I walked in and they moved," she said again. "They moved away from me . . . and I heard Linda say, Call the police. Nobody said anything to me, I don't think. I kind of like screamed, like this huge scream like *nooooo*!!!! and the gun went off. I just remember one time and one noise, but I know that I must have done that [she pulled an imaginary trigger] because you have to do that on the gun, but it was so fast. I just went *aaagghhh*. I felt like I made a huge scream, but I don't know if I made any noise. It was just—just all sensation. I moved in, and they moved . . . then there was this huge explosion and scream and everything all at once."

Did she remember pulling the trigger? "No," she said. She didn't actually remember the gun clicking on empty, either. "I just remember this huge noise and then there was no more noise." As she had the year before, Betty insisted she had not aimed the gun. Her next memory was of pulling the phone out of the wall and running down the stairs, but she insisted she didn't remember seeing Dan or hearing him say anything.

Betty admitted that her daughter Lee reported her repeating Dan's comment, "Okay, you shot me," but she insisted she had no memory of either his comment or of saying that to Lee. Still, she said she accepted her daughter's version because "I know Leelee says I said that, so I must have said that."

Jack Earley ended his questioning, and Kerry Wells got her second chance at Betty Broderick. It wasn't friendly. Referring to Betty's comment that she hadn't been able "to tell anyone how sorry I was," Wells cited the list of interviews she had given from jail, none of which had expressed any remorse.

Point by point, the prosecutor tried to pin down the apparent contradictions in the defendant's testimony. Betty admitted telling a reporter of Dan's last comments, but repeated that she didn't remember them herself, she was recounting what Lee had told her she had said. Betty denied telling a jail deputy during the first trial that when she cried, "the jury would eat it up."

At times, when Wells asked her a question, Betty just agreed, responding, "If you say I said it, I said it."

Wells pounded away on the fortuitous appearance of the key ring with the "funny looking" key. Unlike her rambling and relaxed, if emotional, answers to Earley's questions, Betty was more careful in her replies to the prosecutor. She explained that the key ring was in a box on the front seat of her van. The whole thing was to be taken to her new condo. "I didn't dig through the box," Betty said indignantly. "It wasn't that big. I just knew Dan had a funny key. There's a funny key. I didn't know if it was the right one."

Betty had said that she didn't start using obscenities until after Dan had moved out. The prosecutor challenged that and forced her to acknowledge that she had frequently and publicly called her husband a "fag." Refusing to back down, Broderick commented, "I probably called him an asshole, too," then added that she didn't think those terms were "bad language."

Although she didn't refer to her late husband in the present tense, as she did during the first trial, there were signs that Betty Broderick still had not fully absorbed the effect of her actions. Kerry Wells was questioning her about throwing a ketchup bottle at Dan Broderick, and Betty explained that she had tossed it as a joke, not a hostile gesture.

"I wish Dan were here to tell you the truth," Betty said. A startled

Wells responded, "Well, I wish he were here, too." And Betty could be heard saying, "So do I."

There were more frequent clashes between Kerry Wells and Jack Earley, most out of hearing of the jury. The sharpest came when the prosecutor asked Betty about abortions. Before the trial, Whelan had ruled that Earley could not mention Betty's nine pregnancies, nor the miscarriages and abortions that ended four of them. The defense attorney objected to the prosecutor's apparent violation of that decision, but Whelan did not take any action on it at the time.

"I had a hard time," Earley said later. "The judge couldn't understand why I wanted to get before the jury that she'd gone through nine pregnancies with this man. He said, 'What difference does that make?' "

The prosecution's cross-examination continued Wednesday morning. Kerry Wells picked out more inconsistencies. The blow that Betty claimed broke her sternum came after she had rammed the front door of Dan's house with her car. It had never been X-rayed, but Betty knew it was broken because "that's what it felt like . . . for a very long time."

Questioned about the push that had hurt her ankle, Betty backtracked slightly about Dan's motivation, saying, "He had a temper. I'm sure he didn't mean to hurt me. I think he was embarrassed that he pushed me down." There were questions about Betty's spending sprees and her repeated comments that she didn't want to be a single mother while accusing Dan of stealing the children.

Kerry Wells introduced individual pages from Betty's diary, although the defense had not been allowed to offer the entire ten volumes. At one point Betty acidly remarked, "If you're going to keep putting in pages of the diary, you should put in the whole diary, which show my day-to-day demise and destruction."

Wednesday's session was cut short when two jurors came down with the flu before noon. By Thursday the bug had spread to Kerry Wells and the trial was recessed until the following Tuesday—Monday being Veteran's Day. It would be Wednesday before the trial resumed session, and Thursday before Kerry Wells began her cross-examination of actions on that fateful morning.

When the trial resumed on Wednesday, the prosecution again spotlighted the apparent contradictions in Betty's version of events. Wells brought out Dan Broderick's considerately worded letters to disprove the accusations he had been manipulative. Betty insisted there were "all kinds of hidden messages to me" that were meaningless to "anyone else in this room."

Her responses to other specifics were equally vague. Betty said that she remembered that Dan had been "playing around" with her support checks in 1987. Kerry Wells produced Betty's own deposit slips for the year, showing checks were promptly deposited at the beginning of each month. Betty answered it was her "recollection" that there had been problems.

She denied her obscene references to Dan and Linda affected her children, defending herself with the comment, "I figured I'm telling them what's going on here." Telling the children to disobey, even hate their father, was okay, she said, because "I didn't think they should be living with him."

Kerry Wells, growing exasperated, pointed out that Betty wasn't nearly as helpless as she had portrayed herself. Betty had expressed herself vehemently to everyone she met, and she had frequently threatened to kill Dan Broderick. Betty's response drew gasps from the courtroom spectators: "I never did anything. Those were just empty threats."

The next day, Wells questioned her about the morning the threats became reality.

WELLS: What did you expect to accomplish by confronting him?

BETTY: I wanted him to give me the kids.

WELLS: And you thought by going to his house and entering his bedroom at five-thirty in the morning, he would be inclined to give you the kids?

BETTY: He would be inclined to listen to me.

WELLS: And you took the gun initially to make him listen to you, not to commit suicide, right?

BETTY: I took the gun to make him listen, if he wouldn't listen, I was going to kill myself . . . So that he couldn't say you've got ten seconds to get off this property or I'm going to call the police, or Linda couldn't yell, as she used to yell out the window, Do you want me to call the police?

WELLS: After a show of force, did you think you would get custody after a gun confrontation?

BETTY: I thought so. I thought I could make him see how serious I was, that I really wanted the kids, like, now. No more playing games.

WELLS: And you went in the back so he wouldn't wake up, so you could sneak up on him, right?

BETTY: I didn't want him to see me before I saw him, so he couldn't call the police.

For more than an hour they dissected those few seconds Betty Broderick had spent in the dark bedroom. They disagreed on how long it was. "I didn't *enter* the room," Betty insisted. "I didn't walk into the room. I opened the door and took one step into the room, just that motion."

Wells tried to pinpoint the changes in Betty's testimony. At the first trial Betty had said she didn't know if anyone had said anything. "I don't remember anyone talking to me at all," she explained. "I just remember that noise coming out. She didn't say it to me . . ."

As for the scream, Betty had an explanation for that, too. "I still don't know if I made any noise," she said. There was "the sensation of screaming. I don't know if I screamed 'stop' or 'no' or just screamed. And I don't know if a single sound came out. There was just a sensation."

She repeated that theme throughout the cross-examination. On hearing the gun clicking: "I don't know what was going on. I heard this humongous noise and what seemed like a flash or something and the gun was empty. I have no recollection of doing"—*[hand outstretched, finger pulling an imaginary trigger]*—"for the first shot or five shots."

Wells wondered about the colorful descriptions Betty had used this time, her "eyeballs turning backwards" and others.

"Maybe I'm explaining it better this year," Betty responded.

"Maybe you're embellishing it better this year," Wells snapped back.

The acrimonious exchange continued.

WELLS: You saw Dan and Linda on the bed?

BETTY: I have no recollection of seeing them at all.

WELLS: How did you know they moved if you didn't see them?

BETTY: I know now who was where and I know that I had the impression then that she was closest to me, but I don't remember seeing . . . I don't know what I saw then and what I know now from the pictures and the testimony and what happened later.

WELLS: It was your testimony that when you entered the room, Linda moved toward Dan, Linda yelled call the police and Dan moved toward the phone. Did you see any of that happen?

BETTY: That's the impression of the whole thing that I have then and have now.

WELLS: So you saw that happen, correct?

BETTY: I don't remember seeing Linda or Dan at all. It was just blurs.

WELLS: An impression that they were moving away from you, right?

BETTY: Yes.

WELLS: What frightened you?

BETTY: I entered about to say something, they said something first, they started to move, and I just panicked. It was not a thought process. I moved, they moved, the gun went off and it was over that fast.

WELLS: You pulled the trigger, that was a voluntary act on your part, right?

BETTY: I don't remember pulling the trigger, no. I was in a totally altered state of consciousness. I already testified I didn't remember driving there. I was scared to death of confronting Dan Broderick, which I always was because he scared me . . . I moved, they moved, the gun went off when I just tensed, like that. *[hands outstretched as if aiming a gun]* I don't remember pulling the trigger, once, twice at all.

WELLS: You're saying you just tensed like that once, tensed like that twice, tensed like that three times?

BETTY: No! I went *aaagghhh!* I don't know if any noise came out. I had a screaming sensation and tensing, but I don't remember doing that even once. It was reflex action on my part. I didn't even point it.

Wells asked a series of questions about the shots that killed Linda.

BETTY: I didn't point it at anything in particular . . . I don't know . . . It was dark . . . I didn't see Linda . . . I couldn't have pointed at anyone's chest . . . I don't remember pulling the trigger . . . I remember tensing up once . . . I don't remember moving my finger.

Then there were more questions about aiming and firing five times. Betty stuck to her story: "I don't know . . . I didn't see them . . . It was dark . . . I know I didn't move the gun."

WELLS: Did you feel the recoil?
BETTY: Consciously, no. I know it bounced around. That's what guns do . . . I did not change aim or move the gun . . . they were moving . . . The gun didn't move, the bed didn't move.

Wells just wasn't buying Betty's version of five shots fired in terror.

WELLS: You testified if the confrontation didn't work, you were going to kill yourself, but they rolled away and yelled for the police and the gun never came up to your head, it went to their bodies, didn't it?
BETTY: It was a reflex action . . . No thoughts involved.
WELLS: And you didn't leave immediately . . . You walked around the bed to pull the phone out of the wall, didn't you?
BETTY: I'm thinking it [the phone] was on the floor . . . I didn't see that furniture . . . I didn't see Dan . . . I didn't see the bed . . . I didn't see Linda . . . For some reason, I was thinking it was on the floor . . . It had a very, very long cord . . . I could have gotten the cord and pulled the phone to me.

The prosecutor quoted from notes taken by defense psychologist Katherine DiFrancesca—part of the files she had received as a result of the Appeals Court decision the previous summer. The notes, made in an interview after Betty's arrest, indicated that she had told DiFrancesca she had seen Dan on the floor next to the bed that morning, had heard him say "Okay, you got me," and had then "hit him on the hand because I didn't get him."

Betty insisted again that she had no memory of seeing anyone clearly that morning, only "dim" shapes and "impressions," and had only repeated what her daughter had been saying. She pulled the phone from the wall because she feared Dan was going to call the police, and reiterated that she "had no idea that anybody was hit."

Betty's cross-examination ended, but there were still surprises to come. The first came during re-direct on Friday. Jack Earley asked Betty if Dan "had done anything to protect the children" from knowledge of his extramarital affair with Linda Kolkena. Then he asked if her ex-husband had discussed "having you killed." Even Betty seemed startled and broke into sobs before saying, "Obviously not."

That produced a series of sidebar conferences out of the jury's hearing. After lunch Judge Whelan decided to clear up any confusion. The question about Dan Broderick hiring someone to kill Betty was stricken from the record. It was not evidence in the case, but an irrelevant allegation.

Whelan also got around to explaining a previous Earley objection. A week and a half after the issue was first raised, the judge told the jury they should also disregard any questions about an abortion. He had made a pretrial ruling forbidding such questions, and stating that the defense attorney's objection to the prosecutor's query "should not be viewed as an attempt by Mrs. Broderick to hide information."

The week's testimony ended with Don David Lusterman, the psychologist who provided jurors with a general picture of the effects on a marriage of one spouse's infidelity. Earley was allowed to introduce Dan Broderick's Marriage Encounter journal finally, but not Betty's.

Katherine DiFrancesca repeated her diagnosis of Betty's problems in an abbreviated trial session Monday. Then the jury was excused while the lawyers argued about the relevance of the testimony that Betty was a battered woman. During the hearing, Jack Earley disclosed the name of the person who had revealed the alleged plot against Betty Broderick. That prompted Judge Whelan to slap a gag order on the lawyers for both sides.

After the trial, Earley explained that the potential witness had come forward after seeing Court TV's coverage of Betty's testimony. So had a second person, who had mailed envelopes for Linda Kolkena to Betty Broderick. Neither was allowed to testify.

Judge Whelan continued the hearings, but barred reporters and cameras. Despite objections from the local news media, the judge sealed the record of the closed session at the apparent request of the prosecution. Betty Broderick and Jack Earley wanted open hearings, raising a possible issue for appeal. Some of what went on became known. The witness under scrutiny was spotted going through the transcript of the previous trial, the testimony marked with long red slashes.

Daniel Sonkin, the Sausalito family therapist, decided to withdraw as a witness. "They went through every single question that Mr. Earley was going to ask me, which was a process I've never experienced in the twelve years I've been doing expert testimony," Sonkin told reporters.

"The district attorney had access to every question that I was going to be asked, and knew ahead of time exactly how to cross-examine me." The result, Sonkin said, restricted his testimony to saying "Mrs. Broderick was simply an emotionally abused woman." That compromise was unacceptable, and "it was not fair to trivialize the issue of battered women in that way."

Deprived of Sonkin, Jack Earley began calling a parade of character witnesses. Once again, women who knew Betty from school activities or charities talked about her mothering skills, her willingness to volunteer, her organizational abilities, and her disintegration after Dan left. Dian Black talked about her friendship with Betty and the events of that terrible Sunday morning.

The final defense witness was a former San Diego police officer turned private investigator. He said he could not remember the particulars of the six shootings he had taken part in. His testimony supported Betty's claim that she didn't remember any details of the shooting. Earley was not allowed to call the gynecologist Betty had consulted about reversing her tubal ligation after Dan began the affair with Linda.

Judge Whelan also blunted the prosecution's threat to bring in the video of Betty's jailhouse struggle with the deputies. He forbid any testimony about the incident. Dr. Goldzband was on vacation, so the judge agreed to allow Dr. Park Dietz to be called as a prosecution witness, but barred the psychiatrist from interviewing Betty in jail. Dr. Dietz was also told not to give his opinion about "whether or not Mrs. Broderick is a truthful person."

Dr. Dietz did tell the jury that Betty Broderick had two personality disorders, histrionic and narcissistic, but he said that she was not mentally ill because "the disorder is not controlling her." The psychiatrist acknowledged he had also found presidential assassin John Hinckley to be mentally competent.

He said Betty Broderick was not suicidal because "she wouldn't want to spoil such a special and perfect thing as herself." Admitting he had never spoken to Betty, Dr. Dietz said he had used trial transcripts, psychological tests, Betty's diaries, and the Marriage Encounter book to form his opinion.

Just before the jury left for a Thanksgiving recess, Kerry Wells played a tape made five years earlier. In the obscenity-laced conversation with Rhett about plans for the approaching holiday, Betty tells her younger son to "go fight. Go beat up Daddy." The tape had not been heard at the first trial.

The final day of testimony brought more controversy. One of the last witnesses was William A. Robinson, a psychiatrist who worked at Las Colinas jail. He testified that he had interviewed Betty a few hours after she surrendered, and she was neither remorseful nor suicidal.

"She did not have the attitude of guilt, she had the attitude of anger," Robinson said. "People who are angry do not kill themselves." He added that Betty had commented that suicide violated her Roman Catholic religion. "She said that pressure had been taken off her," he said. "She was just happy."

In a sharp exchange with Jack Earley, Robinson admitted that he had seen Betty Broderick in a therapist-patient relationship but felt free to discuss her case because that relationship was over. He was no longer bound by confidentiality, the jail psychiatrist said.

The final prosecution rebuttal witness was also familiar with the Las Colinas jail. Sheriff's deputy Maria McCullough recalled Betty returning from court after her testimony in the previous trial, saying, "I had the jury eating out of my hands." McCullough said the defendant showed no remorse, but "was excited, like a child would be."

Kerry Wells began her closing argument with an easel and a posterboard bearing a blowup from a page of Betty's diary. As she talked, the jury could see the words in Betty's handwriting:

> There is no better reason in the world for someone to kill than to protect their home, their possessions, and their family from attack and destruction. You have attacked and destroyed me, my home, my possessions, and my family. You continue to repeatedly attack and steal and destroy, you are the sickest person alive. A law degree does not give you the license to attack and destroy, nor does it give you immunity from punishment. No one will mourn you.

Wells went through the evidence, pointing out the most flagrant contradictions and inconsistencies in Betty's testimony: "You don't point a .38-caliber gun that you know is loaded with hollow-point bullets at two people just inches away without intending to kill them. That's murder . . . This is not panicked conduct. This is intentional, calculated, deliberate, incredibly cold conduct."

The prosecutor was also furious with Betty's rationalization to her eldest daughter: "Talk about a guilt trip to lay on a child for the rest of your life, to say, 'I killed your father for you.'" Kim wasn't responsible, Wells said, nor was anyone else. Only one person bore the responsibility for the deaths of Daniel Broderick and Linda Kolkena.

"No one but Elisabeth Broderick caused that trigger to be pulled," Wells argued emotionally. "And she pulled it again and again and again and again . . . Did she commit first degree murder? Absolutely."

Jack Earley also had a prop for his closing argument. He placed a metronome on the edge of the witness stand. Its steady ticking, he said, symbolized the "drip, drip, drip" of Daniel Broderick's psychological attack on Betty.

"It goes on and on," he pointed out. "The sound is enough to drive you crazy after you hear it over and over and over again." He argued that his client was guilty of no more than voluntary manslaughter.

"We've all been placed in situations where the things you worked for were thwarted," Earley pointed out, "not because of fairness or right, but because of a bully or because of your race or some other minority status . . ." Dan Broderick had tried to discredit his wife and protect his own reputation, the defense attorney insisted.

If he was really concerned about a threat from Betty, why didn't he get a real security system on Cypress Avenue, Earley asked, instead of hiring guards? "He wanted to announce, 'World, I have a crazy wife,'" Earley suggested. "He doesn't even hook up a security system, because a security system doesn't stand on a corner and wear a badge . . . it's silent, the world doesn't see it, so to him, it was just no good."

Earley's closing argument took up most of the day. Wells presented her final rebuttal on Thursday, begging the jury to reach a decision this time. "You know the people's position is first degree murder. You know the defense position is voluntary manslaughter. We are giving this case to you to make the call. Just make the call."

This time Wells also suggested Betty's motivation for shooting Linda Kolkena. There was "no way she would kill Dan Broderick and leave Linda Kolkena as Mrs. Dan Broderick with all the money," Wells said. "[Betty] thought of it as her money. [She] would make sure if one died, it was Linda. If Dan survived, he'd be miserable, he might even come back to her. That's why she shot Linda first and came back and shot her in the back of the head."

In one change from the first trial, Wells conceded that Dan Broderick had not been the best of husbands: "No one should ever leave their wife. No one should ever leave their husband. It's rotten, and in a perfect world, it wouldn't happen." She also admitted that Linda Kolkena "was not a perfect human being," but "murder is murder. Going over to someone's house and killing them in their bed is murder, and justice demands she be held accountable for that."

Judge Whelan spent forty-five minutes giving the jury instructions in California law. He told them they could choose between first or second degree murder, voluntary or involuntary manslaughter, but "you cannot accept a guilty verdict on a lesser crime unless you have unanimously found the defendant not guilty" of first or second degree murder. Further, he warned them, "you must not be influenced by pity for the defendant or by prejudice against her."

The jury began its deliberations just a few minutes before noon on Thursday, December 5, 1991, and more than seven weeks after the opening arguments. After three days of discussions, they asked to see the transcripts of Betty's testimony about the events on the morning of the shootings. Consulting with the attorneys for both sides, Judge Whelan decided to have the court reporter read back the relevant testimony to the jurors sitting alone in the courtroom.

One day later the jury filed back into the courtroom to announce their verdict. They found Elisabeth Anne Broderick guilty of two counts of murder in the second degree. Betty sat expressionless as the verdict was read, but a tiny smile could be seen when the victims were named. *California* v. *Broderick* was finally over.

EPILOGUE

KERRY WELLS CLAIMED A VICTORY. SO DID JACK EARLEY. HIS FEELING of triumph was probably more legitimate. Twice, the prosecutor had failed to make her case for first degree murder. Twice, Earley had kept his client from a sentence of life without parole.

"You have to understand that the jury's verdict means that the jury bought our defense," he said. "They just did not give it as much weight as we wanted them to do. If the jury had not bought our defense and said Dan Broderick was a wonderful man who was taken advantage of by this woman they would have come back with a first degree in five minutes."

Wells had a different view: "The verdicts or the results were actually very similar. The first time around, there was initially a ten-two split . . . This time around, it was the same split . . . ten very strongly for murder and two holding out for manslaughter, and the alternates, again, were for murder. The first time around, it was just who happened to be sitting in the box. I had fifteen people up there, and thirteen out of the fifteen would have voted for murder."

When sentence was passed in February 1992, Judge Whelan chose the maximum term of fifteen years to life for each murder count plus two years for possession of the gun, to be served consecutively. He announced his decision after hearing emotional appeals from Kerry Wells, from Linda's sister, and from relatives and colleagues of Dan's. Betty Broderick would have to serve at least eighteen years in prison before being eligible for parole.

The trial was ended, but the story wasn't over.

Two weeks after Betty's sentence was handed down, a decision was reached on the future of her two sons. Permanent custody was granted to Dan's former sister-in-law, Kathy, living in Englewood, Colorado. They had been living with her for the past two years and would continue to do so, although she had divorced their uncle Larry and was no longer related to them.

Betty was still fighting to get permission to speak to them. She had hoped one of her brothers would be awarded custody. Instead, one condition of the final agreement was a weekly phone call from her. On the first weekend after the settlement, Betty tried to call Danny for his sixteenth birthday. When that didn't work, she called a newspaper reporter to complain that Kathy Broderick had changed the phone number without telling her.

The TV movie about the Brodericks aired at the beginning of March 1992. It was based on information provided by Dan's brother Larry and Linda's friend, Sharon Blanchet. There was no mention of an affair with Linda, but Betty, played by Meredith Baxter, was seen burning Dan's clothes, vandalizing the house, and making outrageous demands. One reviewer noticed "there is no way this could be the story of a Betty Broderick who twelve people found to be a sympathetic figure."

The problem with the prosecution's argument for first degree murder was its lack of inner logic. The cold-blooded, materialistic, greedy woman described by the state's witnesses would not have deliberately killed the man providing her with nearly $200,000 a year. That vicious, evil, hate-filled person would have known it was much more painful to keep Dan and Linda paying her monthly.

By shooting Dan, Betty was left without income or property. The money remaining from her divorce settlement after legal fees paid for her defense in the first trial. For the second, she was at the mercy of

210

the county and Jack Earley, who wanted to defend her again. It is difficult to believe that the domineering, unemotional, selfish shrew in the prosecution's scenario would act against her own best interests to that extent.

Judging someone else's emotional distress is never easy, but there are some clues to Betty's probable feelings besides her own words. Until Dan had walked out, Betty's life was a model of reliability and predictability. She showed no aptitude for experimenting, for trying new attitudes, or even for stretching her position in life. She was content marrying young, having children, and providing support and stability to her family.

The uncertainty after the separation and divorce would hit such a person much harder than it might someone else. Betty wanted safety and security, assurance that tomorrow would be much like today and the next year would resemble the ones that had gone before. The unasked-for advice from well-meaning friends to put the past behind her and get on with her life would make her angry. The only life she had known or wanted was in tatters through no action of her own. Her anger was immense, but everyone around her was telling her to put it aside and move on.

Betty believed in the great American fantasy: If I am a good person, nothing bad can happen to me. In her mind, she had not done anything to deserve her fate; it had been imposed on her by someone else.

It is not fair to make judgments about someone else's feelings or emotions. No one can know precisely how another person feels. Besides, a judgment is influenced by current attitudes, and those can change quickly. Especially when it comes to judgments based on gender.

New perspectives are providing new insights. The white, middle-class, male-dominated interpretation of emotions, attitudes, and actions is slowly changing with the increasing numbers of experts who are neither white nor male nor middle class.

In the mid-seventies, psychologists decided that boys were naturally more aggressive, while girls were more passive. The experts had observed toddlers separated from a toy in a playpen by a plexiglass shield. Boys tried to push it down while the girls usually sat down and cried until someone came to their rescue.

Barely a generation later, the findings had a new interpretation. Boys were still seen as aggressive, but their shoving didn't accomplish anything. The girls who cried were no longer viewed as passive, however. Their tears brought a mother who lifted them over the barrier. The girls had solved the problem by asking for help while the boys pushed futilely.

Which is not to say that Betty Broderick had found a solution to her problem. She didn't. She took two lives without cause. Nothing can excuse her actions or justify the deaths of Dan and Linda.

But someone may understand a bit better, and in understanding, prevent another tragedy. There were certainly enough signs that Elisabeth Broderick was not handling Dan's desertion "appropriately," to use the psychological jargon. Her escalating acts of vandalism and violence, the refusal to obey court orders or respond to legal demands of hearings, the total change in her personality and appearance were all screams for help that went unheard.

Even after two trials and her sentencing, Betty Broderick seemed oblivious to what she had done. Speaking by telephone to a *Los Angeles Times* reporter, she again demonstrated a lack of awareness of her role in the deaths of Dan and Linda: "It wasn't like I planned to go kill anybody and now I'm sorry, because I never planned to kill anybody."

Under no circumstances can Daniel Broderick be said to have provoked his own death, any more than a rape victim can be said to have brought on the attack by her actions or clothing. But no one knew Betty better than Dan. No one was in a better position to recognize the changes she was going through and to act responsibly. He was not only her husband of sixteen years, but also a trained physician.

Even Kerry Wells agreed after the trial that Dan Broderick had not behaved to best advantage. "I don't think he had the intent to drive his wife crazy," she said. "I think he was in love with Linda, and I think he felt committed, not necessarily emotionally committed to Elisabeth Broderick, but committed to the fact that they were married and they had four kids and he was raised a Catholic . . . I think he felt tremendously guilty about having an affair with Linda and not exactly knowing what to do about the situation . . . I don't think the way he handled the affair was the right way to do it, but I don't think it was maliciously intended. That's my personal opinion."

From the moment the case hit the headlines, the Broderick family and its circumstances were compared with pop culture symbols from television and the movies. Their early life sounded like "Leave It to Beaver." The drawn-out divorce became another *War of the Roses.* Betty's actions were a reverse *Fatal Attraction* or a variant of *Thelma and Louise.*

TV and movies are modern mythology. To find an apt comparison for Betty Broderick, the search should include ancient mythology as well. The Greeks told the tragic story of Medea and Jason. That is the tale that most resonates with Betty's.

Like Betty Broderick, Medea helped Jason overcome enormous difficulties and achieve wealth, fame, and success. Like Dan Broderick, Jason decided he was in love with a younger woman. Medea, in revenge, sent her rival a poisoned robe, then killed the two sons Jason had fathered. The ancient storytellers believed Medea was justified, for the myth ended with her escape on a chariot sent by the gods. Jason died an outcast.

Modern America has different values than the Bronze Age bards and their audience.

A future America may learn to recognize the signs of mental instability or a potential for explosive violence better than we do now. Another generation may better understand the corrosive effects of anger. A time may come when any act of destruction is seen as proof of mental illness, and treatment, not punishment, the rational response.

Dan and Linda are not forgotten around San Diego.

Reidy O'Neil's bills itself as an "Irish Bar & American Grill." Located in the downtown area, its financial backing came from Dan Broderick and his friends. At the door a sign reads: "If you're lucky enough to be Irish, you're lucky enough."

Wood wainscoting lines the walls, brass chandeliers gleam overhead, the carpeting carries a shamrock design, and Irish music plays over the loudspeakers. Framed posters and photographs line the walls: John F. Kennedy, the Boston Celtics, turn-of-the-century Irish immigrants, the movie *The Quiet Man,* and in one corner, Dan and Linda.

A few blocks away, in the San Diego County Bar Association Building, a portrait of Daniel T. Broderick III presides over a third-floor room used for meetings and meals. Brass plaques list those who contributed to the portrait and a memorial fund in Dan's name. The money collected paid for a memorial in an art and heritage center in Ireland.

There is also a memorial of sorts in the San Diego County library. The California Room files include a huge folder labeled THE BRODERICK FAMILY. It contains newspaper articles about the divorce, the murder, and both trials. It is probably not the way Dan Broderick wanted to be remembered in his adopted city.